G000277733

THE PRESTONIAN LECTURE

SCOUTING & FREEMASONRY
two parallel organisations?

by

A.D.G. Harvey
PPrGReg, ProvGMentor (Derbyshire)

Worshipful Master
Authors' Lodge No. 3456

Past Master
Pioneer Lodge No. 9065
Walesby Forest Lodge No. 9674

Member
The Derbyshire Lodge of Installed Masters No. 8509
Notts Installed Masters Lodge No. 3595
Venturer Lodge No. 7897
Austral Lodge No. 2534

Honorary Member
Athenaeum Lodge of Research No. 7455
Durban Installed Masters Lodge No. 9642

National Volunteer with The Scout Association

Carrfields Publications

First published 2012 by
Carrfields Publications
Carrfields House, Long Eaton, Nottingham NG10 2BY
www.prestonian2012.org.uk

Reprinted 2013

ISBN 978-0-9570927-0-9

The proceeds from the sale of this publication
will be divided between
The Masonic Samaritan Fund
www.msfund.org.uk
and
The Scout Association's
Archives Development Project
www.scouts.org.uk

Printed in Great Britain by
Colourstream Litho Ltd
Pride Park, Derby DE24 8JN
01332 224860

Contents

Illustrations

William Preston
1742 - 1818

William Preston and the Prestonian Lectureship

The Prestonian Lecture, the only official lecture held under the authority of the United Grand Lodge of England, is named after William Preston, the foremost Masonic educator of the late eighteenth and early nineteenth century.

Having been born and raised in Edinburgh, Preston moved to London in 1760 where he was initiated in 1763. Preston undertook an in-depth study of the Craft and travelled extensively to further his research. In 1772 he published his findings as "Illustrations of Freemasonry". In the preface to the second edition (1775) he explained his motives:

> "When I first had the honour to be elected master of a lodge, I thought it my duty to inform myself more fully of the general rules of the Society; in order that I might be able to explain to the brethren under my direction, their utility and importance; and OFFICIALLY to enforce a due obedience to them."

In 1774, Preston proposed a course of catechetical lectures on all the degrees of Freemasonry. Also in that year Preston joined Lodge of Antiquity (then Lodge No. 1 but now Lodge No. 2). On the day he first attended as a member he was elected Master. During his three and a half years as Master the membership of the Lodge grew considerably. He became active in the work of Grand Lodge, eventually becoming Deputy Grand Secretary. A dispute with Grand Lodge led to his expulsion for ten years before he was readmitted.

William Preston died in 1818 and was buried within the precincts of St Paul's Cathedral. In his will he bequeathed a sum to Grand Lodge, to provide for the annual delivery of a lecture based on his system of instruction, the lecturer to be appointed by the Grand Master. The lectures started in 1820 but later fell into abeyance.

In 1924 the Lectureship was revived and, apart from a break from 1940 until 1946, a lecturer has been appointed each year since. He is charged with delivering a lecture on a Masonic subject of his choosing, to "instruct and entertain a general Lodge audience". The list of brethren so honoured, and the titles of their lectures, appears at the end of the Masonic Year Book.

Where it all began

Robert Baden-Powell on Brownsea Island
1st August 1907

Introduction

"If it be your will, let us go forth from here fully determined that we will develop among ourselves and our boys that comradeship, through the world-wide spirit of the Scout Brotherhood, so that we may help to develop peace and happiness in the world and goodwill among men."

With these words, Robert Baden-Powell, founder of the Scout Movement and newly proclaimed Chief Scout of the World, closed the first "World Jamboree" on 7th August 1920, less than two years after the end of the First World War. With these same words, repeated almost seventy years later, a Brother Scout started a conversation that awoke my interest in another Brotherhood. That conversation led to my initiation as a Freemason – while wearing Scout uniform – into Pioneer Lodge, the Scout Lodge of Derbyshire, and ultimately to my being appointed to the Prestonian Lectureship.

In this Prestonian Lecture I identify some of the key parallels, and differences, between Scouting and Freemasonry. I explore the influence that Freemasonry might have had on Robert Baden-Powell, the founder of Scouting. I examine major contributions that Freemasons have made towards Scouting and I call upon you to do what you can to support the world's largest youth organisation. While some of the Masonic content will already be well known to members of the Craft, I trust that you will bear with me so that I can the better illustrate the parallels with Scouting.

The parallels

My first parallel concerns the foundations of both organisations.

The history of speculative Freemasonry before 1717 is unclear. However, in that year four private London Lodges met to form what became the world's premier Grand Lodge. Over the next few years, a Grand Lodge structure was developed and this Grand Lodge assumed authority over the private Lodges, with Provincial Grand Masters being appointed to rule locally. The course of development during the eighteenth century was not always smooth, but in 1813 the United Grand Lodge of England (UGLE) was formed from the union of two Grand Lodges, known as the Ancients and the Moderns. Today there are approximately 255,000 Freemasons in England and Wales in Lodges under UGLE, with another 150,000 in Scotland and Ireland. Worldwide there are estimated to be around six million Freemasons.

The Scout Movement also evolved from the bottom-up. Lt Gen Robert Baden-Powell *CB*, the hero of Mafeking and an Edwardian celebrity, wanted to test his ideas for developing in young people a sense of citizenship and purpose, using recreational means. In 1907 he ran an experimental camp on Brownsea Island in Poole Harbour, Dorset. He took twenty boys from very different backgrounds and, in his own words, "Mixed them up like plums in a pudding". The camp was very successful so, encouraged by his friend, the publisher C. Arthur Pearson, Baden-Powell published his ideas about self-reliance, independence, teamwork and morality in a fortnightly pamphlet, "Scouting for Boys". Young men and boys read it, formed themselves into Scout Patrols and followed the instructions contained within the pamphlets. They recruited schoolteachers and other local worthies to become their Scoutmasters. Within weeks Baden-Powell had set up a national office and started putting in place the support structures needed for a growing Movement. In 1909, on the occasion of his investiture as a Knight Commander of the Royal Victorian Order at Balmoral, he accepted the King's suggestion that he devote all his time to Scouting and so resigned from active service with the British Army. He was acclaimed as "Chief Scout of the World" on 6th August 1920 by the Scouts assembled at the first World Jamboree in Olympia. Today there are over 500,000 members of The Scout Association in the UK, with 34,000 waiting to join, and 28 million worldwide.

So, in the case of both Freemasonry and Scouting, early members chose to join together to form something bigger and stronger, and be part of its increasing success.

Perhaps the major parallel, known to all who have been members of both organisations, is that Freemasonry and Scouting are founded on similar moral principles.

The first and foremost membership requirement of each organisation is that those who join must profess a belief in a Supreme Being. Freemasonry was originally specifically Christian, but de-Christianised over the hundred years following the formation of the first Grand Lodge. Scouting has never been exclusively Christian. By not requiring a member's Supreme Being to be specifically the Christian understanding of God, both Freemasonry and Scouting became attractive to people from around the World. Each also became a place where people of different faiths could meet in fellowship and harmony, with shared moral values, despite their religious, social, cultural and national differences.

Indeed, at around the time of the Coming of Age Jamboree in 1929, the Roman Catholic Archbishop of Westminster, HE Cardinal Bourne, suggested that only Scouting could have succeeded in bringing the leaders of the world's major religions together around one table.

The second moral principle shared by the two organisations is service to others. Each organisation expresses this value in its own way. Freemasonry requires every Initiate, to, and I paraphrase here, "Pledge yourself that you are prompted to solicit those privileges [of membership] by … a sincere wish to render yourself more extensively serviceable to your fellow creatures." Later, on being raised to the third degree, his obligation is largely concerned with service to others.

One of the ways that Freemasonry gives service to others is via its second great principle, "Relief". Much of the relief that Freemasons give is the practical, but largely unseen, support to those in distress. Relief also refers to charitable giving, often enabling recipients to use their skills and resources to provide help to others. In 2008 the Freemasons Grand Charity agreed to donate £500,000 to The Scout Association to support the development of new Scout Groups. I will expand on this later in this Lecture.

Scouting teaches service to others in both its Promise and Law. A Scout promises to "Help other people" and, in the UK version of the Scout Law, learns that "A Scout is friendly and considerate." Ever since the publication of "Scouting for Boys", Scouts have been taught the value of the daily good turn. The Rover Scout section, introduced for older Scouts, was built on the principle of service. Furthermore, in UK Scouting, today's "Balanced Programme", or badge scheme, contains many requirements and opportunities for a Scout to offer service to others. This might range from the cliché of "helping old ladies across the road" to digging water wells for villages in Africa. A recent independent study by PACEC showed that Scouting builds lasting networks that develop commitment to oneself, one's peers and the wider community.

The third moral principle they have in common is to look after and develop oneself. Again, this is expressed in different terms. Freemasonry offers personal development in the form of a moral and intellectual journey of self-improvement. The degree structure and ritual of Freemasonry emphasises the Mason's growth as he progresses from ignorance to enlightenment. This is reinforced by the Craft's third great principle, "Truth". This principle can be understood in many ways, but many of us interpret it as striving for high moral standards and as a search for personal truth and self-knowledge.

In Scouting, one learns to always "Do your best" and to "Be prepared". In the UK the stated Purpose of Scouting refers to "The development of young people in achieving their full physical, intellectual, social and spiritual potentials." The UK version of the Scout Law, in common with that of most Commonwealth countries, teaches that, "A Scout has self-respect and respect for others". The Balanced Programme is built around a number of "zones" of personal development.

These moral principles are summarised, in the case of Freemasonry, in the Charge to the Initiate and, in the case of Scouting, in the Scout Promise.

In progressing from the first to the second degree, the Entered Apprentice Freemason learns that Freemasonry is described as "A peculiar system of morality, veiled in allegory and illustrated by symbols." This bewildering explanation simply means that Freemasonry has a distinctive moral code, and communicates this through stories and symbols. Scouting has its own moral code, expressed in the Scout Law. Baden-Powell used stories, or yarns, to communicate his messages,

3

Scouting for Boys
Published in 1908 in six fortnightly parts

Masonic donations to local Scouting

especially throughout "Scouting for Boys". Scouting also uses symbols, especially in its uniform, badges and emblems.

Freemasonry and Scouting have both called themselves Brotherhoods. In Freemasonry we accord each other the title "Brother" whenever we refer to each other and our first great principle is "Brotherly love".

The term "Brother" is not now used within UK Scouting, nor is it in some other countries such as Australia and New Zealand, now that girls can join from the age of six. However, the positive principles underneath the term still apply. Brotherhood is about belonging together, a family sharing what is important to them and supporting each other. In the UK the part of the Scout Law that once said, "A Scout is a brother to all Scouts" now reads, "A Scout belongs to the world-wide family of Scouts". The meaning is the same, even if the language has changed.

One implication of both Freemasonry and Scouting being open to people of all faiths was the increasingly international appeal of each organisation.

The Grand Lodges in England, Scotland and Ireland initially warranted Lodges overseas, largely thanks to the spread of the Empire and overseas trade. In time, countries formed their own Grand Lodges. Masonic harmony is maintained by a series of mutual agreements between the recognised, or Regular, Grand Lodges. Unlike Scouting's "World Organisation of the Scout Movement" (WOSM), there is no global umbrella body in Craft Freemasonry. We refer to Masonry Universal, the connection between those of us who, anywhere in the world, are united by the principles and values of Freemasonry. Nowadays, these "ties that bind" have been of tremendous value in supporting international relief efforts and in providing safe haven to those who need it.

From the start Scouting rapidly spread overseas, first to parts of the then British Empire, then to Chile and to seven other countries by the end of 1909. Baden-Powell referred to Scouting being a force for peace in "Scouting for Boys" and, in 1911, referred to Scouting as, "a practical vehicle for promoting peace between nations." By the first World Jamboree in 1920, Baden-Powell, an old soldier totally horrified by the slaughter of a generation during the First World War, wanted Scouting to be seen increasingly as an international Movement for peace. In 1939 he was nominated for the Nobel Peace Prize. Unfortunately, the onset of the Second World War meant that no Prize was awarded that year.

At the time of writing there are more than 28 million Scouts in 216 countries. In 2007, just 100 years after that experimental camp on Brownsea Island, the UK hosted the 21st World Scout Jamboree at Hylands Park in Essex, when 40,000 young people from almost every country in the world came together to confirm the relevance of, and continued need for, that original message.

An example close to home will illustrate this parallel. A Masonic friend's daughter fell ill while on holiday on the other side of the world. Through Masonic connections she had a visitor at her hospital bedside within the day. Her visitor was a friendly face who was able to provide moral and practical support at a time of great need. That many people could tell a similar story, by substituting its Masonic context with a Scouting one, only serves to strengthen the parallel.

Perhaps one of the strongest parallels between Scouting and Freemasonry is that both require their entering members to take, and all their members to reaffirm, an Obligation (as in the case of Freemasonry) or a Promise (as in the case of Scouting). In each case this oath is a personal statement of belief and commitment. And in each case the entering member becomes a member at the point of making that oath.

In the UK version of the Scout Promise, the member says, normally in the presence of his own Scout Group:

"On my honour, I promise
That I will do my best
To do my duty to God and to the Queen
To help other people
And to keep the Scout Law"

Incidentally, there are simpler versions for members of the younger Sections and alternative forms for those members from other faiths and national allegiances. The essential point is that the intent remains the same, irrespective of "colour, class or creed".

The Freemason's first-degree Obligation requires a Candidate to make a promise, in the presence of the Supreme Being and the members of the Lodge, to keep their honour and to obey a moral code. A Freemason is also expected to obey the "Laws of the state which may for a time become the place of your residence or afford you its protection, … never losing sight of the allegiance due to the Sovereign of your native land." Freemasonry's commitment to charity and Brotherly love parallels the Scout's Promise to help other people.

The Scout Promise refers to the Scout Law. I have already made a number of references to this statement of Scouting values. The current UK version of the Scout Law reads in full:

1. A Scout is to be trusted.
2. A Scout is loyal.
3. A Scout is friendly and considerate.
4. A Scout belongs to the world-wide family of Scouts.
5. A Scout has courage in all difficulties.
6. A Scout makes good use of time and is careful of possessions and property.
7. A Scout has self-respect and respect for others.

Careful analysis of this statement alongside Masonic ritual will see many further comparisons:

1. Trust is a principle referred or alluded to throughout the ritual, especially when a man is made a Mason, takes his obligation and is entrusted with the secrets of a degree.
2. Loyalty is particularly emphasised in the addresses to the Master, Warden and Brethren following an Installation and investiture of Lodge Officers, and whenever he is called upon to show fidelity.
3. A newly made Mason is called upon to be friendly and considerate in the charity charge delivered after his Initiation.
4. A Mason certainly belongs to a world-wide family, or brotherhood, and is welcomed into such at various points at his Initiation.
5. A Mason is called upon to show courage in all difficulties when he is asked to "avoid[ing] fear on the one hand and rashness on the other" and to "steadily persevere".
6. Making good use of time is a key message in the First Degree working tools and when the Mason is asked to "make a daily advancement in Masonic knowledge", as is being careful of possessions and property when the Mason is reminded to act "without detriment to myself or my connections".
7. Showing self-respect and respect for others is implicit throughout the ritual, especially in the Charge to the Initiate.

There are two rather more visible parallels between Scouting and Freemasonry. First, both use handshakes different from those in normal everyday use.

As Freemasons we know that our handshakes are linked to the various degrees to which a Mason belongs. The handshake, or more properly the grip or token, is a means of recognising another Freemason of the same degree and "Serves to distinguish a brother by night as well as by day". The need for this extends back to Operative traditions, when trained Craftsmen were required to prove their qualifications, or degree, to each other when moving from site to site and long before widespread literacy made the use of written certificates possible.

Scouts greet each other with a left handshake. It was believed that this practice originated with the then Major Baden-Powell's experiences with the Ashanti tribe in 1896. According to this story, the Ashanti greeted people with a left handshake because to do so would involve them laying down their shield and therefore trusting the newcomer. However, in a letter to the Revd F.W. Porter, dated 18th October 1931, Baden-Powell himself dispelled this myth and confirmed that the left handshake was chosen simply to be different from the right and to allow Scouts to identify each

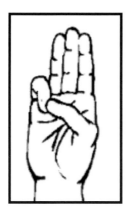

Scout signs & symbols:

The World Membership Badge
The left handshake
The Scout Sign

other.   Later correspondence in The Scout Association's archives indicates that the Ashanti would never use a left handshake.

So, like in Freemasonry, the Scout handshake is distinctive and is used simply to identify another member.

The second of these visible parallels is the way both organisations use salutes.   As Freemasons our system of salutes are physical expressions of the various Masonic degrees.   Again they are used to prove a Mason's qualifications and also as a mark of respect to a senior Freemason.   Of course, other salutes and signs are also used in other parts of our ceremonies.

Scouts salute with three fingers, representing the three parts of the Scout Promise. These are:

1. duty to God and to the Queen
2. help to other people
3. keeping the Scout Law.

The Scout salute is used as a mark of respect at the hoisting of National flags, at the playing of National Anthems (when in the presence of the Sovereign), to Scout flags and to funerals.   When taking the Scout Promise, Scouts make the Scout Sign.   This is similar to the Scout Salute but the hand is kept to level with the shoulder.

I have made reference to a Freemason progressing from one degree to the next.   As he progresses through each degree the Freemason faces a test of his merit, takes another obligation, is entrusted with the signs, tokens and words of that degree and attends to a new moral story.

Scouting is also built on a system of progression.   In the UK, the six-year old Beaver Scout earns first their Membership Award and then completes a series of Challenge Badges before earning the Chief Scout's Bronze Award.   When they progress into the Cub Scout Pack, at the age of eight years, they complete the Moving On Award and further Challenge Awards, culminating in the Chief Scout's Silver Award.   This system continues, through the Scout Section, between the ages of ten and a half and fourteen years, up to the Queen's Scout Award which can be earned, either by Explorer Scouts, between the ages of fourteen and eighteen years, or by members of the Scout Network, up to the age of twenty-five.   At all stages the awards reinforce the four areas of personal development and the values and principles of Scouting.   At each stage the Scout is tested and has to prove their merit.   Indeed, the Boy Scouts of America call their awards, "Merit Badges".   Having proved their merit, Scouts are presented with their new award in a short ceremony, while those who achieve the highest accolade have the honour of attending the annual Queen's Scouts' parade at Windsor Castle.

Unlike Freemasonry, Scouting does offer direct entry for people to join at any age after the minimum. When a young person joins in this way, the skills and experience they bring with them are recognised and accredited within the award scheme.

Adults in Scouting complete a structured training programme relevant to their role, but they do not follow any progressive award system. Nor, in the UK at least, do they wear badges of rank or appointment. The training scheme for adults does recognise and accredit their prior learning and achievements, where relevant and appropriate to the needs of Scouting.

Both organisations confer their own honours or awards for valued service. In Freemasonry a Lodge may elect a brother its Master or to be an honorary member. The Provincial Grand Master may honour brethren with provincial grand rank, just as the Grand Master may honour brethren with grand rank.

Scouting also recognises adult good service over many years. It does so by bestowing one of four national awards, namely the Chief Scout's Commendation for Good Service, the Award of Merit (for outstanding service), the Silver Acorn (for specially distinguished service) and the Silver Wolf (for service of the most exceptional nature). Other countries have a similar system of Good Service awards. For example, Australia has the Silver Kangaroo and Japan the Golden Pheasant. Other honours can be awarded for meritorious conduct or gallantry. All good service and other awards are made nationally, which in the UK is by the Chief Scout.

Two further parallels between the two organisations relate to personal freedom. Both Freemasonry and Scouting avoid becoming involved in party politics, which are considered to be divisive, while nevertheless encouraging its members to contribute to civic matters.

Freemasonry's position is stated in paragraphs six and seven of its document, "Aims and Relationships of the Craft" :

"6. While English Freemasonry thus inculcates in each of its members the duties of loyalty and citizenship, it reserves to the individual the right to hold his own opinion with regard to public affairs. But neither in any Lodge, nor at any time in his capacity as a Freemason, is he permitted to discuss or to advance his views on theological or political questions.

"7. The Grand Lodge has always consistently refused to express any opinion on questions of foreign or domestic State policy either at home or abroad, and it will

Gateway to the 21st World Jamboree
Hylands Park, August 2007

Queen's Scouts' Parade
Windsor Castle

UK Adult Awards for Good Service

HRH The Duke of Kent
MW Grand Master &
President of The Scout Association

HRH The Duke of Connaught & Strathearn
MW Grand Master &
President of The Boy Scouts Association

not allow its name to be associated with any action, however humanitarian it may appear to be, which infringes its unalterable policy of standing aloof from every question affecting the relations between political parties, or questions as to rival theories of government."

The UK Scout Association's policy is defined in its "Policy, Organisation and Rules", Rules 14.1 and 14.2 (b) which state:

"14.1 (a)   The Scout Movement is not connected with any political body.

"14.1 (b)   Members of the Movement in uniform, or individuals when acting as representatives of the Movement, must not take part in any party political meetings or activities that endorse any particular political party or candidate.

"14.2 (b)   In pursuance of the Association's Purpose, each Member of the Movement shall, within the bounds of age and mental maturity, be encouraged:

☐ to become involved in the processes by which decisions are made within the Association and, to that end, to understand the organisation of the Association;
☐ to become more aware of major social issues at local, national and international level;
☐ to understand the processes of decision-making by organisations and by government, and to become aware of the individual's role in such processes."

The Scout Association itself has actively lobbied the UK parliament on issues relevant to volunteering and parliamentary select committees have, in turn, sought its views on such matters. The "All Party Parliamentary Scout Group" was formed in 1946 as the "Houses of Commons and Lords Scout Club" by the then Chief Scout, Lord Rowallan, and Baden-Powell's son, Peter, the Second Baron Baden-Powell. It brings together parliamentarians across different parties and both Houses, to address parliamentary matters in a Scout-like manner. It also holds an annual reception for Scouts in Speaker's House, helping to educate young people in the political process and institutions. In June 2011, MPs worked alongside Scout Leaders to run a Cub Pack meeting in the Houses of Parliament, as a means of promoting Volunteer Week.

Freemasonry seeks to make its own decisions on a consensual basis and to maintain harmony in all matters. Scouting encourages young people to share in decision-making at each level of its organisation, from the Scout Group to national headquarters.

The countries in which the organisations do not exist are usually non-democratic. Indeed, both organisations are repressed by totalitarian regimes, whether left or right wing. When Fascist dictators took power across Europe during the 1930's, they outlawed both Freemasonry and Scouting, although they both tended to go underground. With the collapse of Russian Communism in the 1990's, and the re-introduction of democracy, both organisations very quickly re-established themselves.

Both organisations are voluntary. Freemasonry asks its candidates to vouch that they are "free men" before they take their Obligation. That is, they have made no prior Obligation to another Master (the traditional meaning), they are free to make their own decisions in life and use their time and resources as they see fit (the contemporary meaning), they are therefore free to enter Freemasonry and they, "Come of their own free will and accord".

When Baden-Powell met with Mussolini in 1933, following the latter's suspension of all Scouting in Italy and his claim that his own youth organisation was an improvement, B-P explained the voluntary nature of Scouting as one of four essential differences between Scouting and Il Duce's "Ballila Youth". Both organisations are led by volunteers, who make policy and strategic decisions, supported by a relatively small number of professional staff, most of whom are employed at national levels.

An interesting parallel is that of diversity. Of the six areas of diversity (Age, Disability, Gender, Sexuality, Race, Religion or Belief), Freemasonry and Scouting have similar approaches to five of them. Both organisations have a membership that comprises people from different races, religions and beliefs and both require members to believe in a Supreme Being. Both organisations take active steps to accommodate disabled members and neither excludes people from membership on the basis of their sexuality. Both have lower age limits, but no upper age limits, for membership.

That leaves only one of the six areas of diversity where there is a difference between traditional Freemasonry and Scouting; gender. I will address this difference in a later section.

A coincidental parallel is that, in the UK, both organisations have, in a senior position, HRH the Duke of Kent, who is both the Grand Master of the United Grand Lodge of England and the President of The Scout Association. He is not the first to have held both offices. Our Grand Master at the time that Scouting started, HRH the Duke of Connaught & Strathearn, became President of The Boy Scouts Association in 1913 and performed the opening ceremony at both the First World Jamboree, at

Olympia in 1920, and the Third, the Coming of Age Jamboree, at Arrowe Park in 1929.

Other Royal Freemasons have also actively supported Scouting and held senior appointments, including HRH Prince Edward, the Prince of Wales and later HM King Edward VIII, who was Chief Scout for Wales, and two of his brothers, HRH Prince Albert, Duke of York and later HM King George VI, who was President of the Scout County of London, and HRH Prince George, Duke of Kent and father of our current Grand Master, who was Commodore of Sea Scouts.

My final parallel is one that can only really be appreciated by someone who has been a member of both organisations. Each person would express it in their own terms and my way of doing so is deeply personal. Scouting gave me my moral basis, the values and code that I have sought to follow throughout my life. It gave me a sense of belonging and purpose through difficult stages in my childhood and adolescence. From Scouting I have learned responsibility, self-reliance and the importance of service to others. Freemasonry has given me a vehicle through which I can develop my understanding of those same values as an adult. It has enabled me to reach a deeper understanding of myself, to develop my sense of purpose and to build an inner strength and resilience. It has also helped me to project that self-awareness outwards in my personal and professional relationships.

In conclusion to this section of my Lecture, while there is no formal or official link between the two organisations (and nor should there be), both are built around similar values and are essentially working towards a similar goal, to make us better people. Furthermore, both have a system of progression, recognition and symbolism. Both have international appeal and serve to bring together people from different national, religious and political allegiances.

Having identified a considerable number of important parallels, I will now examine some of the key differences between the two organisations.

Some differences

My first key difference is that Scouting has always been essentially a youth Movement. While it seeks to develop adults, the focus of that development is to provide leadership and guidance to young people between the ages of six and twenty-five.

Freemasonry is substantially different. It requires its members to be of mature age, able to make their own decisions in life. It also requires them to already have

Girl Scouts at the
Crystal Palace Rally, 1909

Red Rose Patrol
1st Poole Girl Scouts
1909

Girl Scouts today

demonstrated that they live by a moral code.   Freemasonry does not offer rehabilitation. It does offer a path through which a good man may become better.

The second obvious difference is that recognised Freemasonry is open only to males, while Scouting in the UK and many other countries is open to both males and females.

Adult women have long been members of The Scout Association. Girls were first able to join Scouts in the Venture Scout Section. In 1991 Scout Groups were permitted to accept girls from the age of six. From 2007 all Groups have been open to both girls and boys in all training Sections. Yet Baden-Powell started a Movement for boys. Once again, as with the founding of Scouting, the members led the way. That girls joined Scouting in its earliest days is well documented in contemporary editions of "The Scout". Twenty-four uniformed girls of the Wolf Patrol were photographed with Baden-Powell at the 1909 Crystal Palace Rally.   Wishing to, in his words, "Do something about the girls", Baden-Powell sought the help of his sister, Agnes, to form the Girl Guides.

The Scout Association's position on this issue is, first, that it is more appropriate nowadays for young people of both sexes to grow up and socialise together and, secondly, that it wishes to be an inclusive Movement, open to all young people who can live by or aspire to its principles and values. Many believe that Baden-Powell, a man of his age who, in 1907, had not spent very much time in the company of women, might well have founded a mixed Movement if he had started it in 2007 rather than 1907. In 1931 he wrote, concerning joint camping and hiking in the older Scouts and Guides sections:

> "I am in favour ... this is all in accord with modern ideas now prevalent. Personally I think it all to the good, especially in our Movement where Rovers and Rangers are sensible and self-respecting young people. The Chief Guide [Olave, Lady B-P] concurs in this opinion."

Scouting nevertheless recognises that many young people will want to spend some of their time in single-sex activities. It is not required that all Scout activities should be mixed.   Girlguiding UK is focused on providing a girl-only environment and is perfectly happy with the developments within The Scout Association that, incidentally, have not adversely affected their own membership figures.

What is the position of Freemasonry on this matter? As it spread around the world, Freemasonry developed a system of mutual recognition between the independent national Grand Lodges. The system was based upon the traditional "Antient Charges" used by the stonemasons' Guilds and, as stonemasonry was historically a male-only occupation, Freemasonry was also restricted to men only. This delicate system still holds the recognised Grand Lodges together. If any Grand Lodge unilaterally opened its membership to women it could no longer be recognised by the others and Masonry universal would be divided. Any change to the system would necessitate a simultaneous concord between all of the world's recognised Grand Lodges. Clearly this could only occur if there were an overriding worldwide consensus for change. This cannot happen while there exist the social, cultural and religious differences in the role of women between the countries involved. Whether it could ever happen at some point in the future is, of course, a matter of conjecture.

In the meantime, there are a number of mixed and women-only Grand Lodges that have been formed within the last hundred or so years. While they are structured in similar ways, practice the same rituals and seek the same truths, they are not officially recognised, nor do they ask to be so recognised, by the wider Masonic brotherhood. Recognised Freemasonry in the UK does have various associations for women and – as we well know - is in no way an anti-female organisation. Indeed, I have heard less chauvinistic talk at Masonic gatherings than at many business or professional meetings.

My last key difference is that whilst Freemasonry, in common with many membership organisations, is currently experiencing a declining membership, Scouting has been growing at an average of four percent per annum since 2005. Why is this?

Both organisations face tremendous challenges in these times of rapid social change. They compete with sophisticated entertainment opportunities for their members' leisure time, while the social climate in which they operate has changed dramatically in the last fifty years. Today, when employing organisations have become less hierarchical and more informal, we are less deferential to those in senior positions, according them respect on the basis of merit rather than position. Our time is at a premium and our employers expect us to be flexible. The language of the media and of the streets is materialistic rather than spiritual. How can Freemasonry and Scouting present themselves as relevant and meaningful against this backdrop?

I believe that Freemasonry is looking for a way to address these issues. Scouting has already addressed them by, first, reaffirming its core principles and purpose and, secondly, by refreshing the way it organises and manages itself, locally and nationally. It has concentrated on providing a quality offering to all its members, including those who have been members for a considerable time. It is now less hierarchical, more flexible and streamlined. It makes extensive use of technology and appoints people to senior positions on merit rather than time-served. It provides award-winning education and training to its adult members. It has extended itself into communities where it did not previously exist, with a lot of help from The Grand Charity.

Scouting found that making these changes was not easy. Some members wanted to hold on to practices and traditions that, while comforting, were actually peripheral to what defines Scouting and makes it worthwhile. Ultimately though, when peripheral traditions cloak the core – that which is really important – and obstruct the future health of the organisation, perhaps it is time to review them and find new ways of offering what makes the organisation so special.

We in Freemasonry know what is at our core. It is our ritual, the principles and meaning it conveys and the way in which we communicate it to each other in our private ceremonies. Other matters – such as meeting times, the handling of business in Lodge meetings, participation in decision making, dining practices – are more peripheral and yet can affect the extent to which good younger men, who might be attracted to Freemasonry, actually become engaged with the Craft. Lodge histories show that many of our Masonic forefathers, like us today, debated these very issues. Those Lodges that were flexible and willing to change the peripheral matters, to suit changing conditions and needs, tended to be the ones that survived. As the saying, attributed to Charles Darwin, goes:

> "It is not the strongest of the species that survives, nor the most intelligent, but rather the one most adaptable to change."

Perhaps if we in Freemasonry today are willing to review and, where we find appropriate and necessary, adapt the peripheral practises in our Lodges – not the core - we might succeed in growing too.

I will now address the question of whether the founder of Scouting, Robert Baden-Powell, was a Freemason and how these parallels, significant despite the differences, might have came about.

Was Robert Baden-Powell a Freemason?

Robert Baden-Powell was born in 1857. A member of a "good family" with strict Victorian values, he was brought up by his mother, Henrietta Grace, after his father, the Revd Baden Powell, Savilian Professor of Geometry at Oxford, died when B-P was just three years old. He followed school at Charterhouse with a direct commission into the 13th Hussars, one of the foremost Cavalry Regiments in the British Army, having come second in the Cavalry Examinations out of around 700 who sat the exam. Most of his army career was spent in India and Africa. He experienced rapid progression to Colonel, at which rank he came to public attention as the Hero of Mafeking, having led the defence of that town for 217 days. He did not marry during

Major General R.S.S. Baden-Powell
Shortly after the Relief of Mafeking
1900

his years in the Army but enjoyed a good social life with his fellow Officers, spending his spare time excelling at sports and in amateur dramatics.

Freemasonry was very popular at this time, especially in India. Many British military men and civil servants joined local Lodges, normally choosing one under the English, the Scottish or the Irish Grand Lodge. For example, Rudyard Kipling was initiated as a Freemason into an English Lodge, Hope and Perseverance Lodge No. 782, in India in 1886. Baden-Powell and Kipling were good friends. They first met in Lahore in the early 1880's and remained close until Kipling's death in 1936. Bro Kipling's writings tell us much about the multi-cultural nature of Freemasonry in India during the period both he and Baden-Powell were there. It would have been entirely natural if Baden-Powell, this sociable "man's man", had joined a Lodge and become a Freemason. Indeed, Alan Cooper suggests, "it was considered in those Victorian days a social essential for gentlemen to become Freemasons".

But for some reason he did not. No record exists in the files of the United Grand Lodge of England, nor in the Grand Lodge of Scotland or that of Ireland, to indicate that Baden-Powell became a Mason. Was it possible that he joined a Lodge under a different constitution? It would be unlikely for a British Officer to do so, given the number of military Lodges available at the time.

Baden-Powell was a prolific writer and many of his writings express similar values and principles to those found in Masonic ritual. For example:

> "Try to leave this world a better place than you found it and, when your turn comes to die, you can die happy in feeling that at any rate you have not wasted your time but have done your best."

And:

> "The repression of self and the development of that love and service for others, which means God within, bring a total change of heart to the individual and with it the glow of true Heaven. It makes a different being of him."

The style is different but the meaning is there.

Perhaps for this reason, many have assumed that B-P was a Freemason. He received two letters of congratulation from Masonic bodies in the days following the Relief of Mafeking. The first, from the District Grand Secretary of South Africa, Western Division, said:

> "I am informed that you are a member of the Craft ... but if my information is incorrect, be assured that our congratulations of admirable skill remain sincere."

The second, from Pollokshaws Royal Arch Lodge, Glasgow, makes a similar assumption. Even in more recent times some have claimed it to be so.

However, no evidence or record of his membership has ever been produced. Nor has any record of his attendance at a Lodge meeting been found. Freemasonry in India and South Africa at the end of the nineteenth century, particularly in relation to the British military, was very well documented. If he had joined or attended a Lodge, surely evidence would have been produced by now.

Baden-Powell's wife, the World Chief Guide, Lady Olave Baden-Powell *GBE*; his secretary, Mrs Eileen Wade; his daughter, The Hon Betty Clay *CBE;* and his grandson, The Hon Michael Baden-Powell, have all confirmed that B-P was not a Freemason - the latter two to me personally.

B-P's younger brother, Major Baden Fletcher Smyth Baden-Powell of the Scots Guards, the Intelligence Officer of the force that relieved Mafeking, was the only one of B-P's brothers to have become a Freemason. He was initiated into United Lodge No. 1629 on 8th July 1914. He was Passed and Raised in Household Brigade Lodge No. 2614 in 1919, becoming a joining member of that Lodge in 1926.

So, if Baden-Powell was not a Freemason, what did he know of and think of the Craft? There is a clear line of evidence that he thought well of it.

First, it is known that Austral Lodge No. 2534 (English Constitution) held at least four Emergency Meetings in Mafeking during the siege, on 18th February, 11th March, 22nd April and 6th May 1900. The meetings were announced in advance in the "Mafeking Mail Siege Slips" (*Produced daily, shells permitting*) and reported afterwards in the same by the editor, Bro GNH Whales. According to the Lodge Treasurer, Bro Edward Ross, the first of these was while the Lodge was:

> "Under a condition of siege, surrounded by the enemy on every side, with heavy artillery pointed at us, and everybody a soldier under martial law, and actually during the time the Lodge was working a volley of Mauser bullets fired into the town."

Baden-Powell, as the Officer Commanding the British forces in the town, had declared Martial Law on 13th October 1899, at the start of the siege. On 3rd February 1900 he clarified for the townspeople the definition of Martial Law as the "legalised abolition of Civil Law and the substitution for it of the will of the Commanding Officer". Taking the law into his own hands, B-P had banned all meetings of local organisations. The Lodge meetings, known as "Siege Lodges", were therefore held with his express permission. Indeed, in his diaries Ross wrote that, although he was not a Mason, B-P had offered to design a special "Siege Jewel" for the Lodge, to commemorate the 200th day of the siege. However, the Lodge has no record that such a jewel was ever created and I have found no sketch amongst the scrapbooks that B-P kept containing his various ideas and designs.

Austral Lodge No. 2534 (EC), Mafeking
Brethren & visitors
Photographed on Sunday 25th February 1900, the 136th day of the Siege and seven
days after the first Siege Lodge meeting

HRH The Duke of Connaught & Strathearn,
MW Grand Master
During his 1906 tour of East Africa
& South Africa

B-P's inscription in Baden Powell Lodge's VSL

As an aside, the then Grand Master, HRH the Duke of Connaught and Strathearn, congratulated the Lodge for continuing to work during the siege when he visited Mafeking on 1st February 1906, during his tour of inspection of East Africa and South Africa in his capacity as Inspector-General of the Forces.   Coincidentally, Baden-Powell, by then Inspector-General of Cavalry, accompanied the Duke of Connaught on this tour and recorded in his diary that he was present with the Duke in Mafeking that day.   United Grand Lodge clearly recognised the siege meetings of Austral Lodge because the Lodge was granted a Centenary Warrant in June 1995, signifying one hundred years of continuous and uninterrupted working.

WBro Cecil Potter, PAGDC, Founding Treasurer of Juventus Lodge No. 6473 in London, wrote in a letter dated 20th January 1966 that he knew Baden-Powell and his son Peter, and that he had personally invited Baden-Powell to become a Freemason.   The founder replied that he was concerned that doing so might offend Roman Catholic Scouts, given that Church's historic antipathy towards Freemasonry. It is of interest to note that B-P's son, Peter, held a similar view, although many of his friends were Masons and often spoke with him about joining.

The first Scout Lodge anywhere in the world was the Baden Powell Lodge No. 488 in the United Grand Lodge of Victoria, Australia. Baden-Powell himself gave permission to WBro Charles "Arch" Hoadley, Chief Commissioner for Victoria, Australia's Contingent Leader to the 1929 World Jamboree at Arrowe Park and the Lodge's subsequent Deputy Worshipful Master, for the Lodge to use his name when the two met during the Jamboree.   The Lodge's founding Junior Warden, Bro William Kennedy, later wrote:

> "Things moved in earnest soon after we returned [from the Jamboree], though there was some difficulty in getting permission to use the name 'Baden Powell Lodge' because it is unusual for a Lodge to be named after a living person".

In fact, the Lodge is thought to have been the first to be allowed to name itself after a person while they were still alive. For that person not to be a Freemason was a signal honour indeed. Since 1930 all States in Australia have formed Baden Powell Lodges.

The Lodge was consecrated on 29th September 1930 by Victoria's then Governor, Chief Scout and Grand Master, MWBro His Excellency Lt Col The Lord Somers *KCMG DSO MC*. Lord Somers was the first Worshipful Master of the Lodge and a personal friend of Baden-Powell.   It was Baden-Powell's wish that Lord Somers be his successor and appointed him Deputy Chief Scout in 1935. Lord Somers was indeed appointed Chief Scout of the British Empire in March 1941, following Baden-Powell's death.

Years later, The Hon Michael Baden-Powell, grandson of the founder and younger brother of the present Lord Baden-Powell, was initiated into Baden Powell Lodge No. 488 and was installed as its Master on 28th September 1998.

On a visit to Melbourne in 1931 Baden-Powell inscribed and autographed the Lodge's Bible. The inscription reads, "With best wishes for the success of the Lodge in its good work. Baden-Powell of Gilwell, 12th May 1931".

Perhaps the strongest evidence of Baden-Powell's favourable opinion towards Freemasonry comes in a letter he wrote as Chief Scout, sent to all 3,550 Lodges in the English Constitution, at home and overseas, and dated 15th September 1921. The letter followed an exchange with the Grand Secretary, Philip Colville-Smith, and a meeting with him at Freemasons' Hall on 15th July. Bro Colville-Smith suggested some minor changes to the wording of B-P's intended letter and advised that it should be posted mid-September, after the start of the Masonic season. In his diary for that day B-P recorded the meeting, and noted that Bro Colville-Smith was, "very sympathetic and hopes they will help our fund unofficially".

In the letter Baden-Powell asked Lodges to support the "Prince of Wales' Boy Scout Fund" and to "lend a helping hand" to the Boy Scout Movement at the "present critical time in its history", when growth was sharp following the 1920 Jamboree but when "the upset of money values since the war has put us in a hole financially". The letter went on to outline Scouting's goals and successes in terms that would appeal to Freemasons. Specifically, B-P referred to giving every boy the chance to become a good citizen, to the "non-political, non-class, non-military and interdenominational" methods Scouting employs and to the goal of "promoting peace and goodwill among the future men in a practical way". He then stated:

> "Our principles are closely allied with those of the Freemason, being those of Brotherhood and Service."

B-P mentioned the support that the Grand Master gave to Scouting, HRH the Duke of Connaught being also the President of The Boy Scouts Association, and enclosed a letter from HRH the Prince of Wales, Chief Scout for Wales.

Given all this evidence, it is very clear that Baden-Powell was well disposed towards Freemasonry and its principles, despite not joining himself. So, if he did approve, was he influenced by Freemasonry in the early years of Scouting and did he draw on Masonic patterns when he created the principles, format and structure of the Movement?

Baden-Powell would have been very aware of Freemasonry. In the late nineteenth and early twentieth centuries Freemasonry was more visible to the public than it is today. The Grand Master and other rulers laid foundation stones in full regalia. Two Masonic periodicals were on sale to the general public via newsagents. The press reported Masonic events. In addition, B-P came into close contact with senior Freemasons, including royalty, his commanding officers and friends. We can only

TELEGRAMS: "SCOUTCRAFT, LONDON"
TELEPHONES: VICTORIA 8654 AND 8655

IN REPLY PLEASE ADDRESS
THE SECRETARY
AND QUOTE.........................

THE BOY SCOUTS ASSOCIATION,

IMPERIAL HEADQUARTERS,

25, BUCKINGHAM PALACE ROAD,

LONDON, S.W. 1.

Sept. 15th, 1921.

Dear Sir,

Prince of Wales' Boy Scout Fund.

I want to ask whether your Lodge would care to lend a helping hand to the Boy Scout movement at the present critical time of its history.

The upset of money values since the war has put us in a hole financially and handicaps us vitally just at the moment when we might otherwise be expanding to do a big work for the country.

I need scarcely remind you that our aim is entirely to make good citizens and to give to every boy, including the very poorest, his fair chance of becoming one.

We are non-political, non-class, non-military and inter-denominational in our methods.

There is no doubt about the attractiveness of the movement to the boy; and the training has been successful in its results beyond all anticipation.

Parents have expressed their gratitude to us for what we have been able to accomplish for their sons; the public, police, and civil authorities have thanked us for their services.

The movement now numbers some 350,000 British and some 1,500,000 Scouts about the world. Our object is to promote Peace and Goodwill among the future men in a practical way.

Our principles are closely allied with those of the Free-mason, being those of Brotherhood and Service.

H.R.H. the Duke of Connaught, your Grand Master, is also President of the Boy Scouts. He takes the warmest personal interest in our progress.

I enclose a letter from the Prince of Wales, who, in his capacity as Chief Scout for Wales, is also closely concerned in our welfare.

Several Masonic Lodges have already responded to His Royal Highness' appeal, and I feel therefore that I have only to bring it to your notice to gain for it the sympathetic consideration of your Lodge.

Should the members desire any further information I should be only too glad to furnish it.

Yours sincerely,

Robert Baden-Powell

speculate about the conversations he may or may not have had with these brethren, and about the influence those conversations had on his thinking.

But it is very unlikely that he did model anything in Scouting specifically on Freemasonry. He did write about and admire chivalric codes, selecting St. George to be the Patron Saint of Scouting. He likened Scouting to the mediaeval ideals of knighthood, telling Rover Scouts specifically, "I look to you chaps to be the knights of the twentieth century". In this he was surely asking them to adopt, and to live by, the noble ideals of chivalry and to serve others.

Superficially, the Rover Scout investiture ceremony, devised some years after the start of Scouting, did share some of the basic characteristics of a Masonic ceremony; namely an introduction into an assembly of Rover Scouts, a series of qualifying questions, the taking of a promise, the presentation of badges and a symbolic story; in this case based upon the legends of King Arthur and his Knights of the Round Table. However, these characteristics are not exclusively Masonic and appear in many other rites of passage. Rather, Baden-Powell is thought to have modelled the investiture, and the preceding vigil, on the admission ceremonies of the mediaeval orders of knighthood, probably the Order of the Bath, and to have refused to introduce more overt Masonic elements into Rover Scouting.

In the United States, in 1915, two Scouters, E. Urner Goodman and Carroll A. Edson, formed the Order of the Arrow within the Boy Scouts of America. Edson was at the time a 32° Scottish Rite Mason. Goodman later became a Mason and went on to achieve his 32°.

The Order was designed with three grades of membership; *Ordeal*, *Brotherhood* and *Vigil Honor*. Each grade had a ceremony that contains elements shared with Masonic ritual; admission and challenge, a pass, perambulations representing a journey, an obligation and modes of recognition used to indicate the grade attained. Parts of the original ritual used language which is recognisably Masonic, though the more overtly Masonic language was removed in 1934. Of course, the Order was founded some years after Baden-Powell defined the purpose, values, form and structure of Scouting.

Other Scouting pioneers were Freemasons. For example, Col David Cossgrove, a Boer War veteran, started the first Scout Troop in New Zealand in 1908 and was appointed Dominion Chief Scout in 1910. His "Empire Sentinels" scheme for older boys was imitative of Freemasonry and was designed to offer "the right kind of knowledge at this critical period of the young man's life". It comprised "three degrees of efficiency", each based on the Scout Promise and following a journey from religious duty in the first degree, through patriotism in the second to self-sacrifice and service to others in the third degree. The ritual included opening and closing ceremonies and meetings were held in "The Watchtower". The office structure was:

Empire Sentinel	Masonic equivalent
Chief Sentinel	Worshipful Master
Sentinel of the South	Warden
Sentinel of the East	"
Sentinel of the West	"
Inner Guard	Inner Guard
Outer Guard	Tyler
Junior Watchman	Junior Deacon
Senior Watchman	Senior Deacon
Scribe	Secretary
Padre	Chaplain

Cossgrove offered the scheme to Baden-Powell, who rejected it as, "it lacked the spirit of adventure". Empire Sentinels did not survive much beyond Cossgrove, who passed away in 1920.

Earlier, in 1914, and for similar reasons, Baden-Powell had turned down a proposal from a Harold Whiston, of Macclesfield, for "a kind of Masonic Brotherhood" within Scouting.

Scouting has always recognised the value of ceremonial. However, Scouting ceremonies today are brief and simple, yet dignified and meaningful, with little of what Freemasons would consider as ritual. While I have heard Freemasonry called "Scouting for Men", because of its shared values, it is certainly not the case that Scouting can be called "Freemasonry for Boys" – or girls.

It is most likely that Baden-Powell drew on an underlying set of principles and ideals that were prevalent at the time of the founding of Scouting. Freemasonry undoubtedly contributed to and was part of those ideals. But it is clear in B-P's writing that he was aware of, and admired, the symbolism and rituals used in many cultures around the world. In creating the values, symbolism and progressive nature of Scouting maybe he was simply recognising the needs people have for a moral code, ceremonial, identity, belonging and achievement. He seems to have modelled certain ceremonial elements on the ceremonies used in chivalric Orders. Perhaps Freemasonry, in its own way and many years before, also developed in response to similar needs and from similar origins.

We have been told why Baden-Powell did not become a Freemason during what he called his Life Number Two; the Scouting years. The question that remains for me is why he did not become a Freemason during what he called his Life Number One; his army career in India and Africa. In those days membership of the Craft was almost a social necessity. B-P's mother, Henrietta Grace, used her extensive family and social contacts to advance the careers of her children at a time when such practices were more acceptable than they are today. He might have been expected to join the Craft, even if only for the perceived advantages it might bring. Yet it appears that none of Henrietta Grace's sons joined the Craft until 1914, just three months before her death.

So much of the Craft would have appealed to Baden-Powell. The values and virtues, the regalia and ceremonial (he enjoyed uniforms, costumes and pageants), the comradeship and formal dining (his scrap books contain many ephemera from school, regimental and dining-club dinners) and even the drama of the ritual (he took part in many plays in his school and Army days). Furthermore, he seems to have had some considerable knowledge of Freemasonry. It is reasonable to assume he would have been sounded out about joining during his Army career, in which case he must have declined. Why did he believe Freemasonry was not for him?

I have read much of B-P's writing. Among the clear messages that come across are his love of the simple, open and active. Did he perceive Freemasonry as mystic, secretive and contemplative? Or was there some other reason why a fiercely ambitious young Army Officer, keen to use networking to further his career, did not seek Initiation? Clearly this is a subject that will merit further research.

Masonic Scouters

If Baden-Powell was not himself a Freemason, was he influenced by others who were – especially at the time when he developed his ideas for Scouting? And what role have Freemasons played in Scouting since then? In this section I will identify some of the Freemasons who have played key or prominent roles within Scouting. For every one listed there are many others; these names are not intended to comprise an exhaustive list but only to be representative.

The most senior Freemason with whom Baden-Powell associated was the Grand Master, HRH the Duke of Connaught and Strathearn. They first appeared to meet in late 1883 after the Duke was appointed Divisional General at Meerut, India. Baden-Powell was a Lieutenant and the Assistant Adjutant of the 13th Hussars. He and his friend, Kenneth McLaren, were often asked to dine with the Duke and they became firm friends. In 1913 B-P named his son Arthur Robert Peter (known as Peter), the first name being after the Duke - who had asked to become the boy's godfather. B-P also appointed the Duke to be the President of the Boy Scouts Association. I have been unable to discover anything about any communications the two surely had about Freemasonry, other than the letter that B-P sent to Masonic Lodges to seek support for the "Prince of Wales' Boy Scout Fund". The Duke of Connaught's opening speech at the 3rd World Jamboree in 1929 expressed Masonic sentiments – without using Masonic language - and finished with the words:

> "If I ask myself the question, 'What does the future hold for our countries and for humanity?', I read in your faces the hope and promise of a better world, and in the light of your eyes is the dawn of a better day."

A sketch by B-P of
WBro Sir Alfred Pickford, PSGD

Ernest Thompson Seton, B-P and
Bro Daniel Carter Beard

Bro Ralph Reader *CBE*

Baden-Powell first met Rudyard Kipling in the mid 1880's. In the obituary B-P wrote for Kipling in "The Scouter" he said that the two were life-long friends. It is well known that B-P used Kipling's "Jungle Book" as the basis for the Wolf Cubs when he and Percy Everett created Scouting's junior section in 1916. Kipling also created the Grand Howl and defined how it should sound. He held an appointment as a Commissioner for Wolf Cubs and was a member of the Scout Council. Masonically, Kipling was initiated in India and served as Lodge Secretary while there. He wrote on Masonic themes, one his best known poems being, "The Mother Lodge". On his return to England Kipling became associated with a number of Lodges. He was a founder of The Builders of the Silent Cities Lodge No. 4948, the Lodge connected with the War Graves Commission, of which Kipling was a member, and an honorary member of one of my own Lodges, Authors' Lodge No. 3456. Indeed, Authors' Lodge received what may have been Kipling's last written communication, an apology for absence from a Lodge meeting dated just before he went into hospital and sixteen days before his death.

At least two of the military commanders under whom Baden-Powell served were senior Freemasons. B-P first met Earl Roberts of Kandahar when the future Commander-in-Chief for both India and South Africa, and the man who commanded the force that relieved Mafeking, was a Major-General in Simla. B-P sent Lord Roberts a copy of the manuscript for "Scouting for Boys" and then recruited him to The Boys Scouts Association's first Advisory Council in 1909. Lord Roberts had served as Senior Grand Warden in United Grand Lodge in 1895. Similarly Earl Kitchener of Khartoum, who succeeded Lord Roberts as Commander-in-Chief for South Africa, was a member of the Council of The Boy Scouts Association from 1911. He had been Junior Grand Warden in United Grand Lodge in 1897.

The people who were closest to Baden-Powell at the time when he was developing his ideas for Scouting do not appear to have been Freemasons. They included the founder of the Boys' Brigade, Sir William Smith; a close friend and fellow officer from the 13th Hussars, Major Kenneth McLaren *DSO*; the publisher and founder of the Daily Express, C. Arthur Pearson; and Pearson's literary editor, Percy Everett. It was Sir William who first suggested to B-P that he rewrite his army manual, "Aids to Scouting for NCOs and Men", to be aimed at boys. B-P became an Honorary Vice-President of the Boys' Brigade and Sir William was one of six people to whom B-P sent his first ideas on "Scouting for Boys". McLaren and Everett were with B-P at Brownsea and both went to on to play key roles in Scouting; McLaren as it's first office manager and Everett as a long standing member of the HQ committee, the first Commissioner of Training at Gilwell Park and a confidant of B-P and his wife. No trace can be found of any of these highly influential figures having been initiated into an English Lodge.

One Freemason who was very close to Baden-Powell was Sir Alfred Pickford, the Overseas Commissioner from 1921 until his death in 1947. During the 1920s B-P considered "Pickie" to be his chosen successor. Sir Alfred had been initiated into Lodge of Harmony No. 438, in Cawnpore, India, in 1912. He joined other Lodges on his return to England and was a founder of Juventus Lodge No. 6473, one of the early Kindred Lodges, shortly before his death.   He was Senior Grand Deacon in United Grand Lodge in 1934.   When offered a peerage in 1929, B-P was said to have suggested that both Everett and Pickford should be considered for honours instead. Sir Alfred Pickford already had a knighthood and Everett was to be so honoured in 1930.

In the United States, the social reformer Daniel Carter Beard had formed the "Society of the Sons of Daniel Boone", while Ernest Thompson Seton had started the Woodcraft movement.   Both Beard and Seton merged their fledgling organisations with Scouting, Seton becoming the Chief Scout of the United States and Beard becoming the first National Scout Commissioner.   The two exerted an enormous influence on the development of Scouting in the USA.   Seton was not believed to be a Freemason but Beard was a member of Mariner's Lodge No. 67 in New York City and gave his name to the "Daniel Carter Beard Masonic Scouter Award", which recognises the service that Freemasons give to Scouting.   The award was created by the Grand Lodge of Pennsylvania and is supported by other Grand Lodges in the USA.   It is approved by The Boy Scouts of America.

The only Chief Scout of the UK Scout Association who is known to have been a Freemason was Lord Somers, the Governor of Victoria, Australia, and Grand Master of the United Grand Lodge of Victoria.   In 1935 Baden-Powell appointed Lord Somers to be his Deputy and he became the Chief Scout of the British Empire following the founder's death in 1941.

As Scouting developed, and the years passed, the possibility that Freemasons might have influenced the early years of Scouting diminished and was replaced by the probability that some Scouts would go on to become Freemasons.

One of the best known of these was the founder of the Gang Show; "A Holborn Rover", Ralph Reader.   Ralph had joined the Scouts at the age of eleven in Newhaven, Sussex, and staged his first shows as a Patrol Leader.   After producing shows on Broadway and in the West End, he first staged the Gang Show in 1932.   He was recognised by World Scouting by the award of the Bronze Wolf; and by the nation by appointment to MBE in 1943, for services to the Royal Air Force; and by promotion to CBE in 1957.   Ralph was initiated into Juventus Lodge No. 6473 in 1956 and became a founder of Red Scarf Lodge No. 8448, a Lodge for those who had been involved in Gang Shows, in 1972.

His Honour Judge Dennis Smith served as Chairman of the Committee of the Council of the UK Scout Association at a very challenging time in its history, from 1968 to 1974.   This was the period just after the implementation of the Chief Scout's Advance Party Report and the fundamental changes it brought to the youth sections and appearance of Scouting in the UK.   While still keeping to the core principles laid down by Baden-Powell, the fresh look and approach was considered necessary to ensure Scouting continued to appeal to young people.   An even more detailed review was completed at the turn of the current century, since when Scouting in the UK has been growing each year. Dennis Smith was initiated into University of Birmingham Lodge No. 5628 in 1943. He became a founder of an early Kindred Lodge, Torch Lodge No. 7236, in 1952 and was appointed a grand officer in 1973.

Gerald Baerlein was a Scouting Commissioner in Manchester when he was initiated into The Quest Lodge No. 5969 in 1948. This Lodge was the very first in the UK to be founded specifically for members of the Scout Movement. Gerald went on to join the staff of The Boy Scouts Association, working at Gilwell Park and playing a major role in the development of Leader Training between the 1950's and 1970's. As Deputy Camp Chief he contributed much to the development of Gilwell Park, the home of Scouting worldwide and now the UK Scout Association's national headquarters, and wrote the report of the Chief Scout's Advance Party that led to the most significant changes in UK Scouting up to that time. Today his memory is kept alive with a room named after him in the White House, the unique slate-walled manor house at Gilwell Park, and by the many people who still remember his warm style as a Leader Trainer. Once based nearer to London, Gerald joined Juventus Lodge No. 6473 and became a founder of another of my own Lodges, Venturer Lodge No. 7897, in 1963. Venturer Lodge meets in Chingford, just down the road from Gilwell Park. The founders had wanted to name the Lodge after Gilwell and the Lodge emblem is the Gilwell axe and log.

Another member of Venturer Lodge who worked at Gilwell Park and who left a lasting mark on Scouting was Ted Gathercole, the Park's woodcarver. Ted was an apprentice under the first carver, Don Potter. He was responsible for creating and repairing many of the best-known Gilwell Park landmarks, including countless versions of the Leopard Gates. Ted carved a Scout Stave for me, complete with my initials, shortly before he died. He was the first initiate into Venturer Lodge in September 1963.

A member of Venturer Lodge who, as a volunteer, made a highly significant contribution to Scouting in the UK was James "Jock" Barr. Jock led one of the largest and most successful Venture Scout Units in the country, Druid VSU, before his appointment as Headquarters Commissioner. He was an inspirational leader of the section and gave it a new lease of life before his tragic early death. He was initiated into Venturer Lodge in January 1979 and remained a member until 1992.

James Murray Napier *OBE* was a senior Freemason and Grand Steward who also served as a Commissioner in London. In November 1925 he was initiated into St Alban's Lodge No. 29, one of the nineteen Lodges privileged to nominate each year a member to serve as a Grand Steward. He held that office in 1932 and went on to be acting Assistant Grand Director of Ceremonies in 1951 and was promoted to Past Junior Grand Deacon in 1967. It was Murray Napier who proposed the first joint Lodge meeting of the then five Kindred Lodges in 1952. He became a founder of Juventus Lodge No. 6473 in 1947, the founding Master of Red Scarf Lodge No. 8448 in 1972 and acted as the Immediate Past Master at the Consecration and Installation of the first Master of Venturer Lodge No. 7897 in 1963.

WBro Gerald Baerlein, ProvAGReg

Bro Ted Gathercole

Bro Jock Barr

A more recent Masonic Scouter who held high office in both organisations was Charles Connal Wilson. Charles was initiated into Buxton Lodge No. 1688 in 1947. He progressed to become the Provincial Grand Master for Derbyshire from 1981 until 1988. At the same time he was the County Commissioner for West Yorkshire Scouts. As Provincial Grand Master for Derbyshire he was the catalyst for the founding of my mother Lodge, Pioneer Lodge No. 9065, as well as its consecrating officer. The Lodge was formed to be Derbyshire's Scout Lodge and to commemorate the Year of the Scout, 1982 – Scouting's 75th Anniversary.

One of the founders of Pioneer Lodge was Clive Bemrose, a former County Commissioner for Derbyshire who had been initiated into Tyrian Lodge No. 253 in 1926. The first initiate in 1983 was John Raymond "Kim" Gale, Deputy County Commissioner at the time but later the County Commissioner for Derbyshire.

To refer to any current Masonic Scouter by name would be invidious. There are so many who deserve recognition but I would not wish to embarrass any that I included, nor upset or disappoint any of the many who would, by necessity, be omitted. Gerald Baerlein was fond of repeating a phrase told to him by Lord Somers:

"One should recognise you are safe in the knowledge of anonymity, until your purpose is recognised by future generations for your progress, drive and influence made at your time in developing others".

So I will refer to three without naming them. The first is a grand officer who wrote much of the World Training Manual published by the World Organisation of the Scout Movement (WOSM). For many years active as a volunteer at Gilwell Park, he was also the Association's authority on developments in adult training outside of Scouting. Then there is the head of the UK Chapter of the World Scout Foundation, a trustee of The Scout Association who has held a number of senior volunteer roles over the last two decades. In those roles he has led some of the most challenging and important - indeed landmark - developments seen in Scouting in recent times. In 2011 he was appointed MBE in the Queen's Birthday Honours List. Finally, I include the brother who directed the very first Gilwell Park course on which I worked as a volunteer in 1985. He became an early mentor in my chosen career and it was only some years later that I discovered that he too was a Freemason. These people continue to give to both Scouting and Freemasonry, enriching both organisations with their talents and their leadership.

Within the Craft there are many active Scouters, and supporters of Scouting, who - in a range of varied roles - are serving their communities by helping young people to grow up to live their lives according to the Scout Law. Freemasons are in a minority within Scouting. They have no power base and hold no majority stake in any Scouting structure. But they are doing their bit to give something back, and are demonstrating the value – and values – of Freemasonry, as well as Scouting, to the young people in their care.

I will now turn my attention to the Kindred Lodges Association, the body formed by the first five Scout Lodges in 1952 and which has grown in size, reach and contribution in the sixty years since then.

The Kindred Lodges Association

The first Masonic Lodge in the UK specifically founded for those with an interest in Scouting, and other voluntary youth organisations, was The Quest Lodge No. 5969, consecrated in the Province of East Lancashire on 25th July 1944. It drew its eighteen founder members, all of whom were or had been active Scouters, from the provinces of East Lancashire, West Lancashire and Cheshire. Within a few years it was joined by Juventus Lodge No. 6473 (London), Pro Juventute Lodge No. 6999 (Middlesex), Quest Lodge No. 7102 (Durham) and Torch Lodge No. 7236 (London).

Members of these five Lodges met together in the library of 25 Buckingham Palace Road, the then Imperial Headquarters of The Boy Scouts Association, on 5th February 1952. WBro J. Murray Napier, AGDC, PGStwd, proposed that brethren from these Lodges hold a joint Lodge meeting at a Masonic venue in London. Eighty-six brethren then met at the Talbot Restaurant, London Wall, on 11th September, to receive a demonstration of the first-degree lectures, given by WBros Grumbridge and Morgan, as well as a paper on "The Origins and History of Freemasonry", given by WBro Cecil Potter, that same Freemason who had once invited Baden-Powell to join the Craft.

Incidentally, some years later Baden-Powell House, by then the South Kensington headquarters of The UK Scout Association, was the scene of a more recent Chief Scout being invited into the Craft. A London Scout Lodge was holding a committee meeting when the Chief accidentally walked in. He was made most welcome but declined to stay and did not join the Lodge.

Since that first meeting of Scout Lodges in 1952, the Scouting and other Lodges connected with youth work have continued to meet each year. In 1978 the Kindred Lodges Association (KLA) was officially formed with the aim, "To facilitate and foster fraternal relations among Freemasons who are or were involved in Youth Work". Since 1979 the KLA has held two Festivals each year; one in the spring around the time of St George's Day and the other in the autumn. Each Festival is hosted by a member Lodge. Those brethren who are entitled to do so wear the uniform of their youth organisation.

The KLA has grown to number thirty-six Craft Lodges in the UK at the time of writing, encompassing Lodges whose members are primarily drawn from Scouting, Boys' Brigade and other youth organisations. It also includes six Associate Member Lodges from Australia and New Zealand and is in contact with Lodges in Canada that have a Scouting affiliation.

In 2010 a Mark Lodge was admitted into membership. The Scout Lodge of Mark Master Masons No. 1907 was consecrated by RWBro Robert Poxon, Mark Provincial Grand Master for Derbyshire, on 31st October 2009. Its expressed purpose is to meet in different Mark provinces to bring together the local leaders of Scouting and Mark Masonry, to help them develop relationships and mutual support. The membership comes from twelve provinces. Any Advancement Ceremonies are conducted at the Installation Meeting. The other meetings are held in uniform and comprise brief Masonic business before the Lodge is closed and the leaders of local Scouting are admitted. They are asked to tell the Lodge and its visitors about the challenges and needs of Scouting in that County or Area. I was privileged to be the Founding Master of the Lodge.

In recent years the KLA has sought to introduce "Freemasonry in the Community" principles into its relations with Scouting. Through openness and by communicating to Scouting an up to date understanding of Freemasonry, the KLA hopes to foster a positive relationship with Scouting at national and local levels.

It began this work by contributing to the development of Gilwell Park, the current headquarters of the UK Scout Association and worldwide Scouting's spiritual home. The member Lodges of the KLA donated the money needed to refurbish Baden-Powell's caravan, given to him as a present from the Scouts of the World at the World Jamboree in 1929, and now kept at Gilwell.

The Kindred Lodges Association also put a team of Freemasons together to help build the 2007 Jamboree site. The team constructed the "Desert Hub", a focal point for four sub-camps. The central point was a pyramid; being one of the world's earliest stone constructions a rather suitable contribution from Freemasons. The notice board beside the pyramid announced that it had been built by Freemasons and displayed the KLA logo, incorporating the square and compasses. It was seen by many of the 42,000 campers and thousands of additional visitors to the site. Among those who showed an interest in Freemasonry's contributions to Scouting were HM The King of Sweden and two past Chief Scouts.

During the World Jamboree itself, on 4th August 2007, 118 Scouting Freemasons, many of them in Scout uniform and 27 of whom were overseas visitors to the Jamboree, attended a special Lodge meeting in Chelmsford, hosted by Venturer Lodge No. 7897. At that meeting the Provincial Grand Master for Essex, RWBro John Webb, congratulated Scouting for its part in developing in young people the same values we uphold as Freemasons.

At its first meeting in Dorset, near Brownsea Island, The Scout Lodge MMM No. 1907 agreed to provide a flagpole to mark the site of Baden-Powell's experimental camp on the Island. On 23rd July 2011 the Deputy Grand Master of the Grand Lodge of Mark Master Masons, RWBro Benjamin Addy, presided at a ceremony at which the flagpole was presented to the Island. Just as the Master of the Lodge, WBro Stuart Goold, broke the flag, a bugler blew the original kudu horn that was used by Baden-

Founders' Jewels from four of the five Lodges that
formed the Kindred Lodges Association

The founders of The Scout Lodge MMM No. 1907,
with the Consecrating Officer, RWBro Robert Poxon,
and the Installing Officer, VWBro Colin Cantrell,
31st October 2009

Plaque to commemorate the KLA's
refurbishment of B-P's caravan, Eccles

The author with Derek Twine, Chief
Executive of The Scout Association, and
WBro Steve Gough, Chairman of the
Kindred Lodges Association (KLA),
outside B-P's caravan, Eccles

The author, a World Baden-Powell Fellow, discussing
"Scouting & Freemasonry" with the Honorary Chairman
of the World Scout Foundation, HM The King of Sweden,
31st July 2007

Powell to open the camp on 1st August 1907. Speaking on behalf of The Scout Association, the Deputy Chief Commissioner for England, Mark Tarry, then thanked the Lodge and Mark Masonry for the gift. The event successfully brought together senior members of Scouting and Mark Masonry, hopefully forming the foundation for a positive, sustainable and mutually beneficial relationship.

The Kindred Lodges Association is currently developing further plans to support Scouting at both national and local level. It also wishes to extend its support to youth organisations to others represented in its membership, especially the Boys' Brigade.

Now let us turn our attention to the future of relations between Scouting and Freemasonry, and how the two organisations could support each other in the future.

Looking forward

Having established the considerable parallels between Scouting and Freemasonry, and the contributions that Masonic Scouters and the Kindred Lodges Association have made in the past, I now want to explore the relationship the two organisations could develop in the future, and whether they could even support each other in some way.

As they are both values based organisations, wishing to make a positive impact on the lives of members, and through them on society, some form of communication between the two, certainly at local and preferably at national level, does seem appropriate.

The leaders of the two organisations are amenable. In 2005 the Chief Executive of The Scout Association, Derek Twine *CBE*, told me that his door was always open to the Kindred Lodges Association. Since then he has always welcomed, and we have enjoyed, a regular dialogue on Freemasonry and Scouting.

Since 2008 I have also met on a number of occasions with the Grand Secretary, VWBro Nigel Brown, to discuss Scouting. From our first meeting he has endorsed and actively supports the development of mutual understanding between the two organisations.

In 2010 we started a series of informal lunch meetings between senior members of both organisations, the purpose being to establish contact, to build relationships at national level and to identify issues of mutual interest. I sincerely hope that this process of contact, communication and sharing of ideas – started at national level – will now continue locally.

In 2011 I asked both Derek Twine and Nigel Brown how they saw the relationship at that time, and what they considered was its potential for the future.

Derek's view was that, in the six years since we first discussed Freemasonry, both organisations had displayed collective openness and a willingness to engage with each other. He recognised opportunities for further development and increased mutual understanding, and wished to continue efforts to demonstrate to Freemasons the value of Scouting. He believed that the two organisations - both founded on a desire to improve people, communities & society and both with similar values - should be obvious collaborative partners, nationally and locally.

VWBro Brown also recognised the value of Freemasons establishing close contact with their Scouting peers, especially those who operate at a similar level. In particular, he saw opportunities to share ideas and experiences with people who understand the challenges each other face, and for acting as sounding boards. He would also like Freemasons to be more visible in their communities, being seen giving practical help to groups such as Scouting. While we have been very generous in giving financial donations, this does not always lead to a better understanding of Freemasonry. In developing relationships with local Scouting, Freemasons could offer skills, facilities, contacts and support – as well as money. The Grand Charity's major donation to The Scout Association has created opportunities for us to do exactly this. I explain how in the next section.

However, first we should recognise that, as two independent membership based organisations, each with its own clear objectives, any formal relationship would weaken that independence. We should also recognise that not all of the members of each organisation will be in favour of supporting the other.

Occasionally members of the Scout Movement have complained about any link with Freemasonry. One such protester was a Harold McCrone of Northamptonshire who, in August 1953, believed that being a Freemason was incompatible with being a Scouter and sought a debate on Freemasonry within Scouting. The Administrative Secretary of The Boy Scouts Association, Col C.C. Goodhind, not himself a Freemason, pointed out that McCrone was the only person who had protested about Scouters being Freemasons and that, "it would be wise to allow members of the Movement to make their own choice as to any activities of this kind that they care to adopt."

Thankfully such complaints are few and far between. In 1994 "The Big Issue" published an article criticising The Scout Association. It implicated Freemasonry, and the Kindred Lodges, as contributing to what it claimed was Scouting's secretive culture. Only one letter expressing concern about Freemasonry's role in Scouting was received from a member of the Association. In the years since I have been promoting links between Scouting and Freemasonry, I am aware of only one complaint received by The Scout Association. I am not aware of any Freemason complaining about Craft support for Scouting.

In looking forward we should also consider the context in which the two organisations exist. Both are facing tremendous challenges as society changes and

WBro Steve Gough, Chairman of the KLA, invests RWBro John Webb, Provincial Grand Master for Essex, 4th August 2007

Inauguration of the Brownsea flagpole with RWBro Benjamin Addy, Deputy Grand Master, Grand Lodge of Mark Master Masons, and Mark Tarry, Deputy Chief Commissioner for England, 23rd July 2011

the lifestyles of potential members alter. The strategies the two organisations adopt to meet these challenges may determine the nature of future relations.

The challenges I refer to include issues of public perception, competition for our leisure time, membership numbers, relevance in a modern world and the structure of local organisations.

United Grand Lodge has responded to these challenges by encouraging us to be open, to connect with and to contribute to our local communities, rather than being remote. Similarly it has encouraged us to look at how we educate and support our members, with the Mentoring scheme being placed as a high priority. Within provinces we are being encouraged to examine the viability and health of small Lodges. New techniques are being used to communicate our fundamental message in a contemporary idiom.

Scouting has faced all of these challenges and is now growing, vibrant and in demand from potential members. It has introduced very successful approaches to retaining and recruiting adult volunteers into a values based Movement, devised accessible means of training people to deliver the Scout programme, given local members the tools to communicate with local media and to promote Scouting within their communities and it has created membership support and information services that keep volunteers informed and equipped to do what is asked of them. Surely we can learn something from what Scouting has achieved.

Similarly Freemasonry has much to offer Scouting. Among our members there are many with highly developed skills and experience in areas that are in demand by Scout Groups, Districts and Counties. Accountancy, planning and organisation, charity management, building, public speaking and the law are just a few of the skills brethren could offer to Scouting without having to make regular weekly, or even monthly, commitments. We could also offer our buildings and facilities to local Scout Groups, for their committee and other meetings, Annual General Meetings and training workshops.

Perhaps one challenge we have to face is one of perceptions. Any Freemason older than me would remember a Scout Movement with big hats and shorts and a rather quaint public image. To "all outward appearances" it has changed much since then, but it still retains its values and continues its good work. What B-P called his "great game" is in safe hands and continues to be supported by his family and successors. Behind the local volunteers running programmes for young people there are highly skilled and well-qualified volunteers and staff providing management and membership support ranging from training, through media & external communications to insurance and trustee services. The PACEC study showed that Scouting developed in adults the soft skills and personal attributes most sought by employers and made a significant contribution to the health of organisations in the public, private and voluntary sectors. Not bad for a quaint organisation.

Similarly Freemasonry today does not accord with the public image that has prevailed in the last fifty years. Again, it retains its values and much of its tradition. But it is open rather than secretive and is following a process of development while also contributing to the greater good.

Scouting has established a momentum for development and a desire to refresh how it operates, so as to make its values and benefits appealing to today's young people. Freemasonry is naturally cautious but can it find a way of balancing its values, rituals and teaching – which are traditional and should be preserved – with modern ways of operating and of communicating with current and potential members? If so, perhaps it too can find a new appeal and start growing again.

So how can we promote a better understanding of Freemasonry within Scouting? An equal challenge might be, how can we develop a better understanding of Scouting within Freemasonry? Lastly, how can we use this understanding for mutual benefit?

As many of us in Freemasonry owe so much of our "infant nurture" to Scouting - perhaps even our personal values, which helped us to find an adult home in Freemasonry - I believe it is reasonable to ask that we consider ways in which we might give something back.

In 2008 the Freemasons' Grand Charity donated £500,000, over five years, to support the growth of Scouting and I will outline what has been achieved so far with that money in the next section. Similarly many Provinces and Lodges have donated significant amounts of money over the years to support local Scouting. Helpful and important though such donations are, sadly they do not always result in a better understanding of Freemasonry among the recipients. If we could supplement financial donations with something that brings our two memberships into direct contact with each other, we may be able to make a difference.

What if every Freemason who ever took the Scout promise gave something, however small, of their time, skills or other resources, to support local Scouting? What if every Lodge considered whether it could offer something, other than money, to assist Scouting in their area? Very quickly local Scouting would become very aware of local Freemasonry. Such offers would help create contacts and relationships that may just develop into something enduring and mutually beneficial.

At Masonic Province & Scout County or Area level I would encourage regular contact, communication and exchange of ideas. Perhaps suitable members could be asked to take on a liaison role. Invites to major events, whether formal, charitable or social, could be exchanged. Speakers could be invited to specific functions. Maybe a first step is for the leaders of the Province and the Scout County, or Area, to meet informally and get to know each other. Contact with local Scouting can be made through me or via the Scout Information Centre at Gilwell Park.

Nowadays most charities that give money to worthy causes make explicit the recognition or publicity they want in return for their contribution. Although as individuals we might feel uncomfortable with this bold approach, it is a practice followed by grant making Masonic Charities. Whether we give money, time, skills or facilities, we can ask the recipients to acknowledge our support in their annual reports, to invite our representatives to their AGMs and open evenings and to tell us how our contributions have been used to further their goals and causes. This will increase contact, build relationships and help develop new ideas and opportunities for the future.

In the next section I will outline some of the ways in which Freemasonry and Scouting have already built local relationships, and the benefits that they have found as a result.

Masonic support for local Scouting

The ways in which Lodges and Provinces support local Scouting is appropriately diverse. There is no one pattern that works across the constitution. The fact that there are wide differences reflects the different relationships and needs in different parts of the country.

Historically the most popular way of supporting Scouting – and other community groups - is with financial donations. All around the country, every year, Provinces and Lodges give large sums of money to support local Scouting, especially when there are special events or projects, such as World Jamborees.

The objective of the 2008 Grand Charity grant to Scouting was to, "enhance the lives of children and young people through Scouting" and to help Scouting grow. In return The Grand Charity wished to improve awareness of Masonic support within Scouting and to create local links.

We know that there are over 35,000 young people who wish to join Scouting but whom Scouting can not yet accommodate, due to insufficient leaders and Groups. The Grand Charity money is administered and dispersed to local Scouting by The Scout Association's Development Grants Board (DGB). The DGB establishes the criteria for making grants and operates checks and balances through local Scout Districts and Counties and through its team of Regional Development Managers. Groups that receive grants are asked to make contact with local Freemasonry. It is for us in our Provinces and Lodges to follow-up this initial contact, to build the local relationships to which I referred in the last section.

So far (2011) the money has helped to start over 360 new sections (Beaver Scouts, Cub Scouts, Scouts and Explorer Scouts) each year, bringing in to Scouting more than 12,000 young people and 2,000 adults. Part of the money has also been used to develop new programme materials, to help Scouters provide challenging,

THE FREEMASONS'
GRAND CHARITY

CASE STUDY
Scouts Association

£500,000 grant to the Scouts Association in 2008

A grant of £500,000 was made to the Scout Association in 2008. The money is being used to encourage more young people to join the scouting movement. 340,000 young people have received new equipment, including games books and similar activity resources, paid for by this grant. The Grand Charity have also helped new scout groups with start-up grants.

The Scout Association provides adventurous activities and personal development opportunities for 400,000 young people aged 6-25.

Personal development means promoting the physical, intellectual, social and spiritual well-being of the individual, helping them achieve their full potential. The Scouts Association believe that young people develop most when they are 'learning by doing,' when they are given responsibility, work in teams, take acceptable risks and think for themselves.

©Scouts Association

©Scouts Association

©Scouts Association

If you would like to find out more about the Scouts Association please visit: www.scouts.org.uk

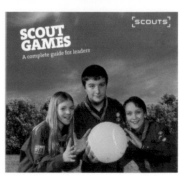

One of the new games books that The Freemasons' Grand Charity has helped to fund.

THE FREEMASONS'
GRAND CHARITY

The Freemasons' Grand Charity, 60 Great Queen Street, London, WC2B 5AZ
T: 020 7395 9261 F: 020 7395 9295 Registered Charity No. 281942
E: info@the-grand-charity.org www.grandcharity.org

adventurous and enjoyable programmes. From 2010/11 a large portion of the money is being used to fund targeted County or Area based activities and projects, agreed between The Scout Association and The Grand Charity, and focused on encouraging and expanding Scouting.

Typically "start-up" grants are used to assess joining lists and potential membership, secure suitable buildings for meetings, tour local schools to recruit young people, brief and train new adult leaders and to provide direct support to fledgling Groups in their first year.

In recent years we have seen the growth of other, non-financial, Masonic contributions to Scouting, including shared social events, exchanged invitations to formal occasions, provision of facilities and offers of skills. As a major organisation Scouting needs people who can help with managerial and administrative matters, as well as those who work with young people. Some of this work requires just a few hours per year; well within the capacity of many Freemasons.

The following examples are intended to illustrate the range of support Freemasons give to Scouting across England and Wales, certainly at the time of writing. There are many further examples that also deserve recognition.

Since "Freemasonry in the Community" week in 2002, Pinewood Lodge No. 8426, has concentrated on supporting the Surrey County Camp Site and donated over £6,000 towards its upkeep and development. Members of the Lodge hold various roles in Scouting across London and Surrey. Three members have been awarded the Silver Wolf for services to Scouting of the most exceptional nature.

In the Province of West Kent the Scout Lodge, North Kent Lodge No. 2499, recently made a donation to help a new Explorer Scout Unit get started. The Provincial Grand Master, RWBro Jonathan Winpenny, arranged for the Province to match the donation. Within a couple of weeks the Unit invited members of the Lodge to attend one of their meetings and to present the Unit with their own Explorer Scout flag. That the Unit members themselves made contact shows their appreciation for the Lodge and creates the hope of future interest, contact and support.

Keeping with the theme of donations, the Province of Lincolnshire has donated a total of £7,900 to local Scout Groups and Districts over four years. Other Lodges within the province have also donated to Scouting to help Groups to develop equipment and facilities.

The Province of Nottinghamshire ran a campaign to raise the money to build a new Reception Centre and offices at the Counties largest camp site, Walesby Forest. Over £75,000 was donated and soon afterwards Nottinghamshire founded its own Scout Lodge, named after the camp site. In 2007, Scouting's Centenary, the Lodge held a special celebratory meeting. Non-Masonic Scouters were invited to join Freemasons in the temple to hear WBro The Hon Michael Baden-Powell deliver a rousing talk. At the meal that followed the Provincial Grand Master, RWBro Robin Wilson, proposed a toast to Scouting in Nottinghamshire. The then County Commissioner, who is not a Freemason, responded by praising the special relationship between Scouting and Freemasonry, its shared values and the time and money invested by many people.

Other Lodges held special celebrations during 2007, including Brownsea Island Lodge No. 9689. It held a Lodge meeting for 150 Masons, in a marquee, on Brownsea Island. Members and other Scouts present renewed their Scout Promise, led by a recording of Baden-Powell. The meeting was made possible thanks to the help and cooperation of the Scout Island Commissioner, a local Scout Group and the Christchurch Gang Show - not to mention the support and flexibility of the Province.

Some Lodges have found rather different ways to connect with local Scouting. After a member of Indaba Lodge No. 9454, in Durham, spoke at a District AGM about Freemasonry and Scouting, the Lodge was asked to give other talks to Scouting audiences in the province. Immediately after that first talk a light hearted conversation led to a challenge; Darlington Scouters versus Indaba Freemasons in an archery competition. The Lodge hopes that this will develop into a regular social exchange and a sharing of ideas.

Members of Warwickshire Scout Lodge No. 9648, together with Shipston-on-Stour Lodge No. 9418, helped the Barford Beaver Scout Colony with its Community Badge. The Freemasons told them about Teddies for Loving Care and helped them develop their own ideas for how they can help those in need.

Woodsmoke Lodge No. 9317, in the Province of Yorkshire West Riding, is organising a "Day Out" for Scout Groups in Bradford and Halifax. The Lodge is also involved with West Yorkshire Scouts "Big Camp" event in 2012, when over 5,000 Scouts will camp at the Yorkshire Showground, Harrogate.

Some Lodges and Provinces have helped Scouting by making available premises and facilities. Both Belper Masonic Hall in Derbyshire and Barnsley Masonic Hall in South Yorkshire are offered free of charge to local Scout Groups for AGM's, social events, committee meetings and training sessions. In Barnsley the local Scouts collect the empty bottles from the Masonic Hall and send them for recycling, all proceeds going to the Scout Group.

In Essex the Provincial Grand Master, RWBro John Webb, has been particularly keen to promote support for local Scouting. He started by inviting Masonic Scouters to attend the Annual Meeting of Provincial Grand Lodge in uniform. The Provincial Grand Master and the County Commissioner have met to discuss co-operation and the Scout County Executive meets free of charge at Chelmsford Masonic Hall. Southend, Upminster, Chelmsford and Braintree Masonic Halls have all made their facilities available to Scout Groups to hold their AGMs and committee meetings, without fee. A number of Freemasons have agreed to serve one or two terms on the

Executive Committees of new Scout Groups, to help them to get established. This has led to the idea of Freemasons acting as mentors to new Executive members and trustees. The province has also offered accountancy support to local Scout Groups. These are excellent examples of time and skills – rather than money - being donated. The Scout County very much appreciates these steps and wishes to encourage the development of relationships with local Lodges.

Another way in which a Lodge has helped with time and skills comes from the Arrowhead Lodge of Freedom No. 8500, in West Lancashire. Through the encouragement of the Lodge, a number of members and visitors have become involved in local Scouting in a variety of uniformed and non-uniformed capacities. Even the Boys' Brigade has benefited as former members rejoined after attending the Lodge. The Lodge also enjoys the distinction of having as one of its Assistant Provincial Grand Masters an active Scouter, WBro Jon Clipsham, PJGD, who has worn Scout uniform as well as his provincial chain to a Lodge uniform meeting. He is one of many Freemasons across the country who hold formal appointments as Leaders, Managers and Supporters within Scouting.

Perhaps one of the most celebrated forms of service that Freemasonry has given to Scouting is the scheme run by Pathfinder Lodge No. 8596, Worcestershire, in the Princess Diana Birmingham Children's Hospital. In 2003 the Master of the Lodge, WBro Malcolm Bird, and his wife, Olwen, who was Birmingham's Assistant County Commissioner for Special Needs, heard about the Scout Group at Great Ormond Street Children's Hospital. Pathfinder Lodge supported Malcolm's proposal to sponsor a Directly Administered Scout and Guide Group at the hospital and the 1st Birmingham (Onaway) Scout and Guide Group was born. Malcolm continues to serve as the Group Scout Leader while the Master of the year is nominated as Group Chairman and the Lodge Secretary acts as Group Secretary. Other members of the Lodge and their wives and partners assist in a variety of ways. Each Thursday evening a team of twelve leaders, Scouters and Guiders, provide a range of activities to four children's wards. Any meeting away from the hospital is held at Pathfinder Lodge's meeting place and much of the fundraising is done through talks given to other Lodges and community groups. Each year the Group AGM is attended by representatives from Scouting, Guiding, Freemasonry and the hospital. All four elements are represented by their respective symbols on the Group badge. The Group is highly regarded and in much demand; in 2010 for the first time it provided over 500 patient nights of activities.

The flow of support is not all one way and already we are seeing Scouting reciprocate. In Chingford, Essex, a Scout Group provides premises for Venturer Lodge's rehearsals. In Nottinghamshire, the Deputy County Commissioner arranged for Scouts to act as Stewards and Marshalls for the Province's 2007 Festival for the Masonic Samaritan Fund. In Norfolk, Scouts are organising a weekend event as part of the Province's 2016 Festival, where they will engage with 500 Freemasons.

The more local Lodges and Scout Groups can build links, and Provinces and Counties or Areas too, the more they will recognise that each has much to offer the other.

RWBro Jonathan Winpenny, Provincial Grand Master
for West Kent, with members of
North Kent Lodge No. 2499 and Explorer Scouts

The Group badge of the 1st Birmingham (Onaway) Scout & Guide Group, based at the Princess Diana Birmingham Children's Hospital

Scouting nationally is a very well organised and sophisticated Movement. It has excellent relationships with the media and a positive public profile. It has management and communication structures, systems and processes that are suited to today's members. It is growing in popularity and reach. Freemasonry, both nationally and locally, can learn a lot from Scouting's experiences.

If these stories represent the range of support given to Scouting within our own constitution, Freemasonry elsewhere also does much to support Scouting.

In other Constitutions

As I explained in an earlier section, the first Masonic Lodge formed specifically for those with an interest in Scouting was Baden Powell Lodge No. 488, Melbourne, Australia, under the Victorian Constitution. The founders of the Lodge had gained Lord Baden-Powell's permission to name the Lodge after the founder of Scouting in 1929. Since then every state in Australia has formed a Baden Powell Lodge, the latest being Baden Powell Lodge No. 1051, New South Wales, consecrated on 9th July 2011.

Other Scouting Lodges have been founded in New Zealand, Hong Kong and Argentina. Scouting enjoys particular support from Freemasonry in the United States of America & in Canada. In Norway there is a growing network of Masonic Scouters. Rather than attempt a comprehensive description of all that Freemasonry is doing to support Scouting around the world - and failing - I will concentrate on Australia and the USA.

Every year since 1997, Baden Powell Lodge No. 488 has presented its "Baden Powell Lodge Rover Service Award" to the Rover Crew in the State of Victoria that the Lodge considers has given the highest standard of service to the community during the previous year. The presentation of the Award is made at the Lodge's annual uniform meeting in the presence of Masons, non-Masonic Scouters and other guests. The opportunity is taken to showcase both Scouting and Freemasonry with tours, talks and camp fires being held at the meeting.

Baden Powell Lodge supports local Scouting in other ways too. As in many parts of the world, its local Scout Training Centre is named Gilwell Park, after the UK Scout Association's centre in Essex. Victoria's Gilwell Park was founded by MWBro Lord Somers, WBro Arch Hoadley and RWBro W D Kennedy, all founders of Baden Powell Lodge. Ever since then the Lodge has supported its Gilwell Park, with time and donations. Its most recent contribution was the provision of a barbecue and shelter.

Another example was the Victorian Grand Lodge's loan of a 4-wheel drive vehicle to the Scouts of Victoria. This followed a simple question from a Past Grand Master of Victoria addressed to Victoria's Chief Commissioner for Scouts. MWBro Dr John Connell *AM* asked John Ravenshall how Freemasonry could best assist Scouting. The

Chief Commissioner explained how the Scouts needed a vehicle to tow its eight metre mobile abseiling tower. The loan of a Ford Maverick was made possible by the then Senior Warden of Baden Powell Lodge, Bro Nick Rinkel, a used car manager. What is significant for me is that senior members of the two organisations met, had a conversation and that a simple question was asked. Everything else followed from these points.

In Western Australia, Baden Powell Lodge No. 350 conducts an annual ceremony to commemorate Founder's Day. The ceremony has the full support of the Grand Lodge of Western Australia, who send a delegation to participate. The meeting is also attended by the Scout Chief Commissioner, members of the Scout Fellowship and Rover Scouts, who have a role in the ceremony itself.

The Lodge has also produced a Strategic Development Plan, linked to its Grand Lodge's own objectives to make Freemasonry more open and attractive to suitable candidates. In the case of Baden Powell Lodge that means Scout Leaders and young men as they leave the uniformed training sections. The Lodge also runs a charitable project, supported by the Scouts Western Australian Branch, called "Assisting Scouts in Need". Through these initiatives the Lodge is succeeding in building its membership and their active participation, particularly among younger Masons.

In Queensland, Baden Powell Lodge No. 505 arranged a pageant to celebrate the Centenary of Scouting in 2007. The event was held in Grand Hall, the home of the United Grand Lodge of Queensland, and was attended by the Grand Master, MWBro Graeme Ewin, his deputy, assistant and a Past Grand Master, the Chief Commissioner for Scouts, Maurice Law *AM*, and the Assistant Chief Commissioner for Guides, Lyn Simpson.

Almost thirty Grand Officers processed in to the meeting, followed by a flag party and the Scout and Guide Commissioners. The cast of the Brisbane Gang Show led the singing of the National Anthem and provided further entertainment. Twenty-one Scouts took part in the pageant, representing the Scouts who attended B-P's experimental camp on Brownsea Island. Four members of the Lodge acted as B-P's assistant leaders while RWBro Eric Summons played the part of B-P. The pageant closed with Australia's first public performance of "The Baden-Powell March", written to celebrate his achievements at the Siege of Mafeking. Senior Freemasons and Scouts, including the Grand Master and the Chief Commissioner, contributed addresses in which they noted the parallels between Scouting & Freemasonry and looked towards the future contribution they each could make, in the words of the Grand Master, "to prepare the Youth of Today to be the Leaders of Tomorrow".

This event was a clear demonstration not only of the parallels between Scouting and Freemasonry, but also of what can be achieved through openness and cooperation. The pageant was a high point in the Masonic and Scouting calendars and created a memorable occasion for those present, including the large number of young boys and girls who took part. Their perception of Freemasonry will, no doubt, be significantly influenced by the experience.

In the United States of America many Lodges and Masonic Associations have supported Scouting. For example, in 2005 in Little Rock, Arkansas, the Scottish Rite Freemasons hosted a luncheon for over 150 business leaders who heard celebrities tell of the value of Scouting. The luncheon raised over $200,000 to help the Quapaw Area Council of the Boy Scouts of America support its membership of over 14,000 Scouts. The local broadcast and printed media carried detailed and favourable news of the event.

Similar stories of support and involvement come from the Grand Lodges of Pennsylvania, Oklahoma, Michigan, Minnesota and Virginia. As well as financial donations, Freemasons have acted as merit badge counsellors (badge examiners), mentors to adult leaders and Council Committee members. Lodges and Masonic Associations have chartered (sponsored) Scout units, with the Grand Lodge of Minnesota adopting over eighty units. Although it has its own youth programme, the Order of DeMolay, American Freemasonry recognises that it has an unusually high percentage of members from Scouting backgrounds and is keen to support Scouting.

The Grand Lodge of Oklahoma worked with the five Boy Scout Councils in the state to create the "Partners in Character Award" (PIC). This is available to Masonic Lodges and Scout sections and is designed to bring the two organisations into direct contact and closer together. To directly quote the programme's own literature:

> "Such a program stands to greatly benefit both Scouting and Masonry. Masonic Lodges are made up of some of the finest people in any community. Their members are some of the best mentors that our youth could ever have. Local Masons for example would make outstanding merit badge counselors. Just think of the amount of knowledge in the average Masonic Lodge. It is a sin not to make the optimal use of these people both as long term and short term mentors."

The award comprises certificates and pin badges, as well as uniform badges for the Scouts.

Another award that is endorsed by the Boy Scouts of America, as part of its "Community Organization Award Program", is the "Daniel Carter Beard Masonic Scouter Award". Created in 2001 by RWBro Dale A DeLozier, District Deputy Grand Master of the 20th Masonic District of the Grand Lodge of Pennsylvania - to honour those Freemasons who have been of outstanding service to Scouting - the award is administered by his Grand Lodge on behalf of all Grand Lodges in the USA.

The award may be conferred on active Scouters who have "displayed outstanding dedication to the Scouting program". Nominees for the award may be recommended by any Freemason but the petition must be supported by both his Scouting and Masonic authorities. The award consists of a certificate, a uniform "square knot" emblem (signifying an adult award) and a silver neck medallion. The presentation

The Grand Master of Victoria with members of Baden Powell Lodge No. 488, all in Scout uniform and Masonic regalia

The presentation of Baden Powell Lodge's 2011 Rover Service Award

The logo of the
National Association
of Masonic Scouters,
United States of
America

The Daniel Carter Beard Award
neck medallion, certificate and
uniform "patch"

may be at a Scouting or Masonic occasion but will always be made by a representative of the award holder's Grand Lodge.

The only non-American Scouter to have been honoured by the award is WBro The Hon Michael Baden-Powell, who received it in May 2007.

Following a special meeting of Fredericksburg Lodge No. 4 - George Washington's mother Lodge - held during the 2005 National Boy Scout Jamboree at Fort A.P. Hill in Fredericksburg, Virginia, two Masons who were present conceived the idea of the "National Association of Masonic Scouters" (NAMS). Brothers David Karp and Wayne Sirmon wanted to continue to meet in a Masonic / Scouting context, and to strengthen the links between two organisations:

> "which promote nearly identical goals with one dedicated to the moral and charitable growth of adult men and one dedicated to the moral, physical and mental growth of boyhood into leaders of the future".

They formed an internet group in December 2005 and in September 2006 advertised in the Scottish Rite Journal, appealing to its readership across the USA. They stated that the purpose of NAMS would be to:

> "foster and develop the support of the Boy Scouts of America by and among Freemasons while upholding the tenets of the fraternity. This includes, but is not limited to, encouraging Masonic Lodges and other Masonic organizations to charter and support BSA units. The NAMS also will encourage the awarding of the Daniel Carter Beard Award to deserving Masons and support the Scouting movement at all levels."

Regular membership would be open to Master Masons who were also active Scouters, while others, including family members, would be able to join as Associate Members.

The Association formally adopted its constitution on 30th May 2007 and was recognised by the Relationships Division of the Boy Scouts of America. It then set out to become recognised by each of the Grand Lodges that have jurisdiction in the USA. Its objectives include the promotion of Scouting within Freemasonry and the appointment of ambassadors (for Freemasonry) to each of the nation's Scout Councils.

This section can only describe some of the many initiatives, partnerships and resultant benefits that Freemasons and Scouters around the world are developing to build links and improve the bonds between these parallel organisations. What works in one part of the world may not suit another. However, it is clear that, where these links are successful, Freemasons are open minded and visible and both the Scouting and Masonic authorities are actively supportive.

In conclusion

I have established that there are clear traditional and contemporary parallels between Freemasonry and Scouting. While it is clear that the founder of Scouting, Robert Baden-Powell, was not a Freemason, it is equally clear that he did hold a very favourable opinion of the Order.

A number of Freemasons have played key roles in the development of Scouting since its earliest days. But Freemasonry did not provide Scouting with its purpose, basis, form or its structure. Today Freemasons continue to serve and support Scouting at all levels of the Movement.

Many Freemasons were formerly Scouts and find in Freemasonry an adult way of expressing the values that they formed through Scouting. Some have formed together into Lodges primarily for those with Scouting affinities and, in England and Wales, the Kindred Lodges Association brings them together in Masonic fellowship. In other constitutions strong relationships have been built between Scouting and Freemasonry at all levels.

While no formal link between the two organisations can - or should - exist, both face a similar challenge; to promote a consistent values-based life-style in a fast changing, largely self-centred and materialistic world.

Both organisations can only benefit from a contemporary understanding of each other; Scouting from the informed good will of former members who are now Freemasons and Freemasonry from an informed "favourable impression, preconceived of the Order" amongst members of The Scout Association.

Such an understanding can best be developed by promoting dialogue, by giving of time, skills & resources - as well as money - and by building relationships between national and local groups of Freemasons and Scouts.

Many Lodges and Provinces are already supporting local Scouting. I ask you now to consider making some of your time, money or other resources available for Scouting; to invest in a Movement that is aligned to our principles as Freemasons and which represents one of the best means available to make people, communities and societies better for us all.

I finish with an un-attributed quotation included in WBro Ron Hall's paper to Pioneer Lodge No. 9065, delivered in 1996.

> "A boy is a person who is going to carry on what you and I have started. He is to sit right where you are sitting and attend to those things that you and I think are so important, after we have gone. We may adopt all the policies we

please but how they will be carried out depends on him. Even if we make leagues and treaties, he will have to manage them. He will assume control of our cities, our provinces, countries and nations. He is going to move in and take over our churches, schools, universities, councils, corporations and government [as well as our Scout Groups and Masonic Lodges]. All of our work is going to be judged and praised, or condemned, by him. Your reputation and future, and mine, are in his hands. All our work is for him and the fate of our nations and all humanity is in his hands."

Once that boy was you and me, but not anymore. Scouting and Freemasonry have both taught me to pay attention to him.

For more information

Further information about Scouting and the Kindred Lodges Association can be found at the following websites:

> www.scouts.org.uk
> www.KindredLodges.org.uk

The Scout Information Centre can put you in touch with Scouting in your area. The telephone number is 0845 300 1818.

The Masonic Samaritan Fund will benefit from charitable proceeds arising from this lecture and the sale of this booklet. By contributing you will help Freemasons and their dependants get the medical, dental, respite and mobility care and support they need. You can find out about the Fund by visiting www.msfund.org.uk.

The Scout Association's national and international archive will also benefit, thus helping to preserve the archive and make it available for future generations. The archive is gradually going online. Visit www.scoutsrecords.org to see what is available already. And please support this vitally important cause by making a gift-aided donation to www.virginmoneygiving.com/prestonian2012.

The Scout Association's "Campfire Circle" is a means of rekindling your contact with the Scout Movement, and keeping up to date with what is happening. Please visit www.scoutscampfirecircle.org.uk to find out more.

Bibliography

1. Adkins, S.M. (2002), "Freemasonry, Scouting and the Order of the Arrow", http://www.100megsfree4.com/stimso/oa1.htm, accessed 3rd August 2011.
2. Anon (1997), "Lord Baden-Powell, Benefactor of Boyhood. B-P and Freemasonry", reproduced by Lewis Orans on www.pinetreeweb.com/bp-freemasonry.htm, accessed 2nd August 2011.
3. Armitage, Keith (1993), "Austral Lodge: The first hundred years", Austral Lodge, Mafikeng.
4. Baden-Powell, Robert (1908), "Scouting for Boys: A handbook for instruction in good citizenship", 2004 edition with an introduction and notes by Elleke Boehmer, Oxford University Press, Oxford.
5. Baden-Powell, Robert (1911), "B-P's Outlook", in The Headquarters Gazette, The Boy Scouts Association, London.
6. Baden-Powell, Robert (1919), "Aids to Scoutmastership", Herbert Jenkins, London.
7. Baden-Powell, Robert (1922), "Rovering to Success", Herbert Jenkins, London.
8. Baden-Powell, Robert (1933), "Lessons from the 'Varsity of Life", C. Arthur Pearson, London.
9. Baden-Powell, Robert (1936), Obituary for Rudyard Kipling in "The Scouter", March edition, The Boys Scouts Association, London.
10. Baden Powell Lodge No. 488 (2011), "About Baden Powell Lodge", http://www.badenpowelllodge.com , accessed 2nd August 2011.
11. Bainbridge, W.A. (1997), "The Best of Both Worlds - Freemasonry and Scouting", Transactions of United Masters Lodge No. 167, Vol. 31 No. 13, Auckland NZ.
12. Bishop, Lionel J. (1940), "A Rover Scout Investiture", Boy Scouts Association Provincial Council for Ontario.
13. The Boy Scouts Association (1946), "The Presentation of a Rover Scout", London.
14. Carr, Harry (1964), "Kipling and the Craft", Ars Quatuor Coronatorum: Transactions of Quatuor Coronati Lodge No. 2076, Volume 77, pp 213-253, London.
15. Connaught, HRH the Duke of (1929), Opening Speech at the 3rd World Jamboree, reproduced by Lewis Orans on http://www.pinetreeweb.com/arrowe-duke.htm, accessed 15th August 2011.
16. Cooper, Alan A. (1987), "The first ten years of Freemasonry in Mafeking / Mafikeng", Austral Lodge, Mafikeng.
17. Cooper, Dennis (1973), "Find the path – from tent to temple", Kindred Lodges Association, London.

18. Cossgrove, Col David (1918), "The Empire Sentinels' Handbook and Ritual", Christchurch NZ.

19. Costello, James C. (2008), "National Association of Masonic Scouters: Creating a new national Scouting affinity group in support of the Boy Scouts of America", College of Commissioner Science, Boy Scouts of America.

20. Edgar, Eric G. (Ed) (2008), "Rudyard Kipling and his Masonic career", http://www.freemasons-freemasonry.com/kipling.html, accessed 15th August 2011.

21. Esplin, Margaret (2010), "David Cossgrove 1852-1920", Dictionary of New Zealand Biography, http://www.dnzb.govt.nz, accessed 4th August 2011.

22. Gombert, Francis (1991), "Origins of Scouting", in "L'Intermédiaire des Chercheurs et Curieux", Number 485, Paris.

23. Goodwin, John R. (1997), "The Order of the Arrow, another Masonic ritual?", http://www.vamason.org/ra1753/papers/1arrow.htm, accessed 3rd August 2011.

24. The Grand Charity (2011), www.grandcharity.org, accessed 4th August 2011.

25. Grand Lodge of British Columbia and Yukon (2011), "Freemasonry and Lord Baden-Powell", http://freemasonry.bcy.ca/texts/baden-powell.html, accessed 2nd August 2011.

26. Green, Jonathan (1994), "Scouts face crisis of confidence", in "The Big Issue", pp27-28, December 1994.

27. Hall, Ronald (1996), "Scouting, Freemasonry and the Kindred Lodges Association", Paper to Pioneer Lodge 9065, Derby.

28. Harris, Steven (2007), "A quirky Biography of Baden-Powell and his Boy Scouts", Lewarne Publishing, London.

29. Hilton, Brian (2000), "The two Brotherhoods – Scouting and Freemasonry", Freemasonry Today, London.

30. Jeal, Tim (2001), "Baden-Powell: Founder of the Boy Scouts", 2nd edition, Yale University Press, New Haven & London.

31. Kendall, George (1984), "Freemasonry during the Anglo-Boer War, 1899-1902", Ars Quatuor Coronatorum: Transactions of Quatuor Coronati Lodge No. 2076, Volume 97, London.

32. Kerr, George W. (1994), "Freemasonry & the Scout Movement", Ontario Mason, Vol. 1.

33. The Kindred Lodges Association (2005), "The Kindred Lodges Association: 1953 – 2005".

34. Library & Museum of United Grand Lodge of England (2011), "The History of English Freemasonry", London.

35. Maris, Leo G. (1982), "Freemasonry and the Scout Movement", Baden Powell Lodge No. 505, Brisbane Australia.

36. The Masonic Illustrated (1901), March, p128, London.

37. Moynihan, Paul (2006), "An Official History of Scouting", Hamlyns, London.

38. Nesham, Robert (1990), "Chaplain's Oration at the Consecration of Impeesa Lodge No. 9385", Impeesa Lodge.

39. PACEC (2011), "A study of the impact of Scouting on the UK's young people, adults and communities", London.

40. Preston, William (1775), "Illustrations of Masonry", 2nd ed, J Wilkie, London.

41. Sica, Mario (Ed) (2006), "Footsteps of the Founder", 3rd (Centenary) edition, WOSM, Geneva.

42. Sica, Mario (Ed) (2007), "Playing the Game - A Baden-Powell Compendium", Macmillan, London.

43. The Scout Association (2011), http://www.scouts.org.uk, accessed 4th August 2011.

44. The Scout Association (2011), "Policy, Organisation & Rules", http://scouts.org.uk/supportresources, accessed 4th August 2011.

45. Sirmon, Wayne & Karp, David I. (2007), "Constitution of the National Association of Masonic Scouters, (April 22, 2007), National Association of Masonic Scouters.

46. Smyth, Frederick (ed) (1990) "Lord Baden-Powell", Ars Quatuor Coronatorum: Transactions of Quatuor Coronati Lodge No. 2076, Volume 103, p264, London.

47. Smyth, Frederick (ed) (1990) "The Scout Movement and Freemasonry", Ars Quatuor Coronatorum: Transactions of Quatuor Coronati Lodge No. 2076, Volume 104, p256, London.

48. Stewart, Greg B. (2010), "Boy Scouts of America, 100 years of being prepared", http://www.freemasoninformation.com/2010/09/bsa100-boy-scouts-of-america-100-years-of-being-prepared, accessed 9th August 2011.

49. The United Grand Lodge of England (1949), "Aims and Relationships of the Craft" in "Constitutions of the Antient Fraternity of Free and Accepted Masons under the United Grand Lodge of England", 2009 edition, UGLE, London.

50. Walker, Colin R. (ed) (2010) "Mafeking Mail Siege Slips", self-published.

51. Walker, Colin R. (2006), "Rudyard Kipling and Baden-Powell", http://www.scouting.milestones.btinternet.co.uk/kipling.htm, accessed 9th August 2011.

52. Whitman, Don (2008), "Partners in Character Award", http://www.pic-award.50megs.com, accessed 8th August 2011.

53. William, B.P. (Ed) (1980) "Edward Ross: Diary of the Siege of Mafeking, Oct 1899 to May 1990", Cape Town.

54. The World Scout Foundation (2011), http://www.scout.org/en/about_scouting/fundraising/world_scout_foundation, accessed 4th August 2011.

Picture Credits

The following illustrations are copyright and are reproduced by the kind permission of:

a. The Scout Association, Gilwell Park (1,3,4,6,8,9,10,11,12,14,20,21,22,23,24,25)
b. The Library and Museum of Freemasonry, London (2,17,19,26,40)
c. The Provincial Grand Lodge of East Lancashire (5)
d. Epping Forest District Council (7)
e. Girlguiding Dorset (13)
f. The Worshipful Company of Mercers, London (15)
g. Austral Lodge No. 2534, Mafikeng (16)
h. Baden Powell Lodge No. 488 (VC), Melbourne (18,37)
i. The Freemasons' Grand Charity, London (33)
j. The Provincial Grand Lodge of West Kent & Bro Simon Gould (34)
k. 1st Birmingham (Onaway) Scout & Guide Group and WBro Malcolm Bird (35)
l. United Grand Lodge of Victoria (36)
m. The National Association of Masonic Scouters, USA (38)
n. WBro The Hon Michael Baden-Powell, Melbourne (39).

The remaining illustrations (27,28,29,30,31,32 & 41) are from the author's own collection.

Acknowledgements

I wish to thank the Trustees of the Prestonian Fund, for honouring me with the appointment as Prestonian Lecturer and for giving me the opportunity to bring my subject matter to a wider audience. I also wish to thank the Board of General Purposes, for nominating me and for allowing me access to the library and records of the United Grand Lodge of England. I sincerely hope I have lived up to the honour and to their faith in me.

I am very grateful to the Provincial Grand Master for Derbyshire, RWBro Graham Rudd *DL*; the Grand Secretary, VWBro Nigel Brown; the Chief Executive of The Scout Association, Derek Twine *CBE*; and the UK Chief Commissioner, Wayne Bulpitt. Each has listened to my ideas for developing a mutual understanding between Scouting & Freemasonry and responded with interest, encouragement and support.

I am indebted to VWBro John Hamill for his support and guidance, and to the following for their patience and assistance with my research:
a. At the Library and Museum of Freemasonry; the Librarian, Martin Cherry, and the Archivist, Susan Snell, and colleagues
b. At The Scout Association; the Archives & Heritage Manager, Daniel Scott-Davies, the Manager of the Development Grants Board, Bruce Murdoch, and colleagues
c. At The Worshipful Company of Mercers; the Archivist, Jane Ruddell
d. At The Freemasons' Grand Charity; the Head of Non-Masonic Grants, Annabel Grout, and the Head of Marketing & Communications, Siobhan McCarthy
e. From Austral Lodge No. 2534 (EC) in Mafikeng; its Archivist, WBro Pine Pienaar
f. and Colin Walker, of Scouting Milestones.

Other friends and brethren have helped and encouraged me as I developed my theme. I am particularly grateful to WBros Peter Carroll, Brian Evangelista, Pat Farr, Steve Gough, Steve Hilditch, Robert Poxon, Steven Varley and The Hon Michael Baden-Powell. In addition, the Secretaries and brethren of the "Kindred Lodges" and other Masonic Associations, in the UK and overseas, have been very helpful and most generous in supplying information.

WBro Trevor Brearley and Mrs Eunice Selby deserve my special thanks; Trevor for designing and developing the website, www.prestonian2012.org.uk, and Eunice for proofreading the manuscript for this booklet. I also wish to thank the members of my Lodges for supporting me in so many ways throughout my "Prestonian journey" and for helping with the charitable fundraising associated with the Lectureship.

In thanking all of the above, I accept full responsibility for any errors.

Most of all I wish to thank my wife Diane, and my daughter Caroline. Without their love, understanding and support I would not be able to devote time and energy to my twin passions of Scouting and Freemasonry.

Deliveries of the 2012 Prestonian Lecture

The Prestonian Lecturer of the year is required to give a number of official deliveries of his Lecture during the tenure of his appointment. Grand Lodge has selected the following Lodges to host the official deliveries of the 2012 Prestonian Lecture:

Authors' Lodge No. 3456, London
North Notts Masters Lodge No. 9525, Nottinghamshire
Humber Installed Masters' Lodge No. 2494, Yorkshire North & East Ridings

In addition, the Prestonian Lecturer may give as many unofficial deliveries as he desires, both during his year and after. The dates and other details of all deliveries are listed on the website, www.prestonian2012.org.uk.

At all deliveries the Lecture is to be the main business of the meeting, with no degree work being conducted.

The Lodges or Masonic Associations that host deliveries are responsible for meeting any reasonable travel and accommodation expenses, so that no costs fall on the Lecturer in carrying out his duties.

The Lecturer is permitted to raise money for his chosen charities by selling the Lecture booklet. Host Lodges and Masonic Associations often donate the proceeds of offertories and raffles to the Lecturer's charities.

The MW The Grand Master has approved a special collarette and jewel to be worn by present and past Prestonian Lecturers as part of their Craft regalia.

Detailed guidance for host Lodges and Masonic Associations is available from Grand Lodge and from the website, www.prestonian2012.org.uk.

Charities supported by the 2012 Prestonian Lecture

I have chosen two charities to be supported from the proceeds of the 2012 Prestonian Lecture. One is a Masonic charity and the other a Scouting one. Both are worthy causes, much deserving of our support.

The Masonic charity is the Masonic Samaritan Fund, which provides grants for medical, dental, respite care and mobility support to Freemasons, their wives, partners, widows and dependants, who have a diagnosed need, face a long wait for treatment on the National Health Service and who can not afford to fund it themselves without incurring financial hardship. Each year the Masonic Samaritan Fund makes grants of over £5,000,000 - more than £14,000 per day. So far no qualifying petitioner has been refused relief due to a lack of funds. However, the UK has an ageing population and Freemasonry an ageing membership. By 2025 it is expected that almost two million people will be over the age of 90 and one million will suffer from dementia. Coupled with cuts in public sector finances, the Masonic Samaritan Fund faces increasing calls upon its resources. Proceeds from the Prestonian Lecture will help the Masonic Samaritan Fund to continue its good work in looking after us and our families when we need it most. More information about the Masonic Samaritan Fund can be found at www.msfund.org.uk. The Fund's registered charity number in England & Wales is 1130424.

The Scouting charitable cause is the development of the UK Scout Association's archives. As the home of the worldwide Scout Movement, the UK has a particular responsibility to protect the many unique and irreplaceable national and international documents and artefacts that date from Scouting's origins to the present day. These documents range from Baden-Powell's handwritten manuscript for "Scouting for Boys" to current plans for growing Scouting's capacity to satisfy the 35,000 young people who are waiting to join. £40,000 is needed to digitise the archive and to move it into a climate controlled environment, compliant with BS5454:2000, preserving it and enabling Scouting's legacy to be shared with a wider audience and future generations. With your support The Scout Association will also be able to complete an archive website to make heritage material available to the public in the UK and overseas. I hope that the proceeds from the Prestonian Lecture will go a long way to meet the cost of this globally significant project. The Scout Association's own funds can then be applied to the growth and development of Scouting, for today and tomorrows' young people. For more information about Scouting in the UK please visit www.scout.org.uk. The Scout Association's registered charity number in England & Wales is 306101. You can donate online via www.virginmoneygiving.com/prestonian2012 or www.justgiving.com/prestonian2012TSA. Both are secure sites.

Thank you for your generous support.

List of Prestonian Lecturers
1924 to 2012

1924. WBro Capt C.W. Firebrace, PJGD, *The First Degree*.
1925. WBro Lionel Vibert, PAGDC, *The Development of the Trigradal System*.
1926. WBro Lionel Vibert, PAGDC, *The Evolution of the Second Degree*.
1927. WBro Gordon P.G. Hills, PAGSuptWks, *Brother William Preston: an Illustration of the Man, his Methods and his Work*.
1928. WBro Dr John Stokes, PJGD, *Masonic Teachers of the Eighteenth Century*.
1929. WBro Roderick H. Baxter, PAGDC, *The Antiquity of our Masonic Legends*.
1930. WBro H.T. Cart de Lafontaine, PJGD, *The Seven Liberal Arts and Sciences*.
1931. VWBro the Rev Canon W.W. Covey-Crump, PGChap, *Medieval Master Masons and their Secrets*.
1932. WBro J. Heron Lepper, PJGD, *The Evolution of Masonic Ritual in England in the Eighteenth Century*.
1933. WBro the Rev Herbert Poole, PAGChap, *The Old Charges in Eighteenth-century Masonry*.
1934. WBro F.C.C.M. Fighiera, PJGD, *The Art, Craft, Science, or 'Mistery' of Masonry*.
1935. WBro Walter J. Bunney, PGStB, *Freemasonry and Contemplative Art*.
1936. WBro Lewis Edwards, PJGD, *Freemasonry, Ritual and Ceremonial*.
1937. WBro the Rev Joseph Johnson, PJGD, *The Inwardness of Masonic Symbolism in the Three Degrees*.
1938. WBro Douglas Knoop, PAGDC, *The Mason Word*.
1939. WBro G.E.W. Bridge, PJGD, *Veiled in Allegory and Illustrated by Symbols*.

1940-6. No appointments were made to the Lectureship during the Second World War.

1947. WBro Gilbert Y. Johnson, OSM, PJGD, *The Grand Lodge south of the River Trent*.
1948. WBro Fred L. Pick, PJGD, *The Deluge*.
1949. WBro Col Cecil C. Adams, MC, PJGD, *Our Oldest Lodge*.
1950. WBro W. Ivor Grantham, OBE, PDepGSwdB, *Lodges of Instruction, their Origin and Development*.
1951. WBro H.W. Chetwin, PAGDC, *Variations in Masonic Ceremonial*.
1952. WBro Bernard E. Jones, PAGDC, *'Free' in 'Freemason', and the idea of Freedom through six Centuries*.
1953. WBro G.S. Shepherd-Jones, PAGDC, *What is Freemasonry?*
1954. WBro Bruce W. Oliver, PAGDC, *The Freemason's Education*.
1955. WBro John R. Rylands, PAGDC, *The Fellowship of Knowledge*.
1956. WBro G.S. Draffen, MBE, *The Making of a Mason*.
1957. WBro Harry Carr, LGR, *The Transition from Operative to Speculative Masonry*.
1958. WBro Norman Rogers, PJGD, *The Years of Development*.
1959. WBro the Rev Canon J.S. Purvis, OBE, *The Medieval Organization of Freemasons' Lodges*.
1960. WBro Sydney Pope, PGStB, *The Growth of Freemasonry in England and Wales since 1717*.
1961. WBro Prof Gerard Brett, *King Solomon*.
1962. WBro P.R. James, *The Grand Mastership of HRH the Duke of Sussex, KG*.
1963. RWBro the Very Rev H.G. Michael Clarke, ProvGM Warwickshire, *Folk lore into Masonry - an examination of the Seventeenth century background*.
1964. WBro the Rev A.J. Arkell, MBE, MC, *The Genesis of Operative Masonry*.
1965. WBro Edward Newton, LGR, *Brethren who made Masonic history*.
1966. RWBro The Hon William R.S. Bathurst, TD, ProvGM Gloucestershire, *The Evolution of the English Provincial Grand Lodge*.
1967. WBro A.R. Hewitt, PAGDC, *The Grand Lodge of England: History of the first 100 years*.
1968. WBro H.Kent Atkins, PAGSuptWks, *The Five Noble Orders of Architecture*.
1969. WBro J.R. Clarke, PAGDC, *External Influences on the Evolution of English Masonry*.
1970. WBro Lt Col Eric Ward, *In the beginning was the Word - An exercise in Ritual Archaeology*.

1971. VWBro the Rev Canon Richard Tydeman, PGChap, *Masters and Master Masonry - A theory of the Third Degree.*
1972. WBro Terence O. Haunch, AGSuptWks, *'It is not in the power of any man' - a study in change.*
1973. WBro C.F.W. Dyer, PAGDC, *'In Search of Ritual Uniformity' - A General Examination of the Regulation and Development of Craft Ritual Procedures after 1813.*
1974. WBro the Rev Neville B. Cryer, PAGChap, *Drama and Craft - The relationship of the Mediaeval Mystery and other drama to the practice of Masonry.*
1975. WBro R. Theodore Beck, PDepGSuptWks, *Anthony Sayer, Gentleman - The Truth at Last.*
1976. WBro Brig A.C.F. Jackson, CVO, CBE, *'Preston's England' - The Everyday Life of Masons in the late XVIII Century.*
1977. WBro Roy A. Wells, PAGStB, *The Tyler or Outer Guard.*
1978. WBro Charles MacKechnie-Jarvis, PSGD, *The Grand Stewards 1728-1978.*
1979. WBro G.J.C. Hambling, DSC, PDistSGW Bombay (vice the late WBro G.E. Walker, OBE, PAGReg, who died on 9 December 1977), *'Who must otherwise have remained at a Perpetual Distance' - 250 years of Freemasonry in India: a study in resolved discords.*
1980. WBro Frederick J. Cooper, TD, PSGD, *Robert Freke Gould: Masonic Historian, 1836-1915.*
1981. WBro Cyril N. Batham, PAGDC, *The Grand Lodge of England according to the Old Institutions.*
1982. RWBro Sir James Stubbs, KCVO, PSGW, *The Government of the Craft.*
1983. WBro Richard H.S. Rottenbury, PAGDC, *The pre-eminence of the Great Architect in Freemasonry.*
1984. WBro Harry Mendoza, *Getting and giving Masonic knowledge.*
1985. WBro Sinclair Bruce, PAGDC, *'... not only Ancient but useful and necessary Officers ...' The Deacons.*
1986. WBro Prof Wallace McLeod, *The Old Charges.*
1987. WBro Christopher L. Gotch, PAGSuptWks, *The Role of the Innkeeper in Masonry.*
1988. WBro Andrew I. Pearmain, PGOrg, *Music and Freemasonry.*
1989. RWBro Sir Lionel Brett, PDistGM Nigeria, *The Constitutions of the United Grand Lodge of England.*
1990. WBro Frederick H. Smyth, LGR, *The Master Mason at Arms - A Short Study of Freemasonry in the Forces.*
1991. WBro Keith Flynn, OBE, *Freemasons at War.*
1992. VWBro the Rev Dr Michael Morgan, PGChap, *Masonry: pure and applied.*
1993. WBro John M. Hamill, PJGD, *'And the greatest of these is charity' - the development of Masonic Charity.*
1994. WBro Michel L. Brodsky, *English Freemasonry in Europe 1717-1918.*
1995. WBro John Webb, PGStB, *Sport and Freemasonry.*
1996. WBro John Goodchild, *Freemasonry and the Friendly Societies.*
1997. WBro R.A. Gilbert, *Freemasonry in popular literature.*
1998. WBro Brian F. Page, PAGDC, *Elias Ashmole - the first recorded English Freemason.*
1999. WBro John F. Ashby, PAGDC, *Freemasonry and Entertainment.*
2000. WBro Richard A. Crane, PGTreas, *For therein you will be taught - some thoughts on the relationship between Freemasonry and Religion.*
2001. WBro Simon Fernie, PAGDC, *The first degree in Freemasonry.*
2002. WBro Charles W. Wallis-Newport, *The Anglo-Irish Masonic connections.*
2003. WBro Prof Aubrey N. Newman, *The contribution of the Provinces to the development of English Freemasonry.*
2004. WBro A. Trevor Stewart, *English Speculative Freemasonry: Origins, themes and developments.*
2005. WBro Gordon W.S. Davie, *Women and Freemasonry.*
2006. WBro Granville S. Angell, *The Victoria Cross - Freemasons' Band of Brothers.*
2007. RWBro Dr Roeinton B.F. Khambatta, PDistGM Pakistan, *The Grand Secretaries 1813-1980.*
2008. WBro Dr R.D.T. Sillett, PJGD, *The Language of the Ritual.*
2009. WBro Dr John S. Wade, *"Go, and do thou likewise": English Masonic processions from the 18th to the 20th Centuries.*
2010. WBro Wayne B. Warlow, *Music in Masonry and Beyond.*
2011. WBro Dr James W.P. Campbell, AGSuptWks, *Was Sir Christopher Wren a Freemason?*
2012. WBro Antony D.G. Harvey, *Scouting & Freemasonry: two parallel organisations?*

The Prestonian Lecturer for 2012

WBro A.D.G. Harvey *FCIPD FCMI FRSA*
PPrGReg, ProvGMentor (Derbyshire)

WBro Tony Harvey is an active Scout as well as a Freemason.

WBro Tony Harvey (right), with WBro The Hon Michael Baden-Powell, grandson of the founder of Scouting (left), 4th August 2007

Joining the Scout movement on his eighth birthday, Bro Harvey went on to become a Queen's Scout.   As an adult he has held appointments at local and national levels. Since the late eighties he has been involved with the work of The Scout Association's UK headquarters where he has been a member of a number of national boards, committees and teams, especially in the areas of adult recruitment, adult training and activities, and has been a regular contributor to Scouting Magazine.   He was involved in defining the Association's future approach to, and standards for, volunteer leadership and management, and during his time as the Prestonian Lecturer was leading a project to develop the way the Association trains its volunteer trainers.

Together with WBro The Hon Michael Baden-Powell, Bro Harvey is a director and trustee of the charity that bought "Jam Roll" back into Scouting.   Jam Roll is the Rolls-Royce car that the Scouts of the World bought for Lord Baden-Powell to celebrate Scouting's coming of age in 1929.   He is both a UK Scout Fellow and a World Baden-Powell Fellow and was awarded The Scout Association's "Silver Acorn", for specially distinguished services, in the St. George's Day Awards of 2006.

Masonically, Bro Harvey was initiated into Pioneer Lodge No. 9065, the Province of Derbyshire's Scout Lodge, in Scout uniform, at the age of thirty-one. He is also a founder and Past Master of Walesby Forest Lodge No. 9674, Nottinghamshire's Scout Lodge; a member of the Essex Scout Lodge, Venturer Lodge No. 7897; and at the start of his Prestonian year was Senior Warden of Authors' Lodge No. 3456 in London, becoming its Worshipful Master during 2012. In 2009 he became the Founding Master of The Scout Lodge of Mark Master Masons No. 1907, a Lodge which meets in different provinces to bring together local Scouting and local Mark Masonry.

Within his home province of Derbyshire, Bro Harvey is the Provincial Grand Mentor and the Mark Provincial Grand Secretary.

As the Kindred Lodges Association's (KLA's) liaison with the UK Scout Association and United Grand Lodge, Bro Harvey meets at intervals with senior staff and volunteers at The Scout Association, to discuss matters relating to Scouting and Freemasonry. In 2008 he was invited to meet with the Grand Secretary, as a result of which UGLE has endorsed Bro Harvey's work. Senior members of both organisations have since met to discuss matters of mutual interest and to build relationships that, Bro Harvey believes, will benefit both organisations in the future.

When he is not engaged in Scouting or Masonic activities, Bro Harvey works as a leadership consultant, trainer and coach. He works with companies and organisations in the private, public and voluntary sectors, designing and delivering bespoke development programmes for directors and managers.

Bro Harvey has published books and articles in the areas of learning, training and organisational development. As well as holding degrees in psychology & education and in management he is a Member of the Institute of Directors and a Fellow of the Chartered Institute of Personnel & Development, of the Chartered Management Institute and of the Royal Society for the encouragement of Arts, manufactures and commerce. He is a Freeman of the City of London and of the Company of Educators.